The
Great
Romantic
Films

Lawrence J. Quirk

THE GREAT ROMANTIC FILMS

The Citadel Press
Secaucus, New Jersey

Also by Lawrence J. Quirk
The Films of Joan Crawford
The Films of Paul Newman
The Films of Fredric March
The Films of Ingrid Bergman
The Films of William Holden

First edition
Copyright © 1974 by
Lawrence J. Quirk

Published by
Citadel Press
A division of
Lyle Stuart, Inc.

120 Enterprise Ave.
Secaucus, N.J. 07094

In Canada:
George J. McLeod Limited
73 Bathurst St.
Toronto 2B, Ont.

Manufactured in the
United States of America by
Halliday Lithograph Corp.
West Hanover, Mass.

Designed by Peretz Kaminsky

Library of Congress
catalog card number: 73-90956
ISBN 0—8065—0401—3

Dedicated to the Memory of My Aunt and Godmother,
MARY CONNERY GORHAM (1885-1957)

ACKNOWLEDGMENTS

Mark Ricci and the Memory Shop, New York; Ernest D. Burns and Cinemabilia, New York; Kenneth G. Lawrence and the Movie Memorabilia Shop of Hollywood; The Staff of the New York Public Library's Theatre and Film Collection, Library & Museum of Performing Arts, New York; Wynn Loewenthal, Warner Bros. Pictures; Hortense Schorr, Columbia Pictures Corp.; Metro-Goldwyn-Mayer, Paramount, United Artists, Universal.

And James E. Runyan, Michael Ritzer, Doug McClelland, John Cocchi.

Table of Contents

Merle Oberon

Introduction

Films dealing with romance, sentiment, love have been one of the staples of cinema literature for over sixty years. I have chosen fifty films dealing with various aspects of romance, covering the years 1932 to 1973. I chose 1932 as the starting point because by that year the sound medium that had made its debut in 1929 had reached a point of polished fluidity, and pictures had taken on a gloss, an esthetic fullness, a technical proficiency that made possible numerous remakes of silent romances which, however admirable in their time and context, were limited by lack of sound and compared to the products of the 1930s on, were crude and perfunctory in terms of thematic development.

The 1925 *Stella Dallas*, for instance, did not compare with the 1937 version for rounded thematic development of the kind to which we refer. And there is a world of difference between the 1922 *Smilin' Through* and the 1932 remake. The same applies to *Alice Adams* (1923 and 1935), *The Enchanted Cottage* (1925 and 1945), *Humoresque* (1920 and 1946). It is interesting to note the technological and esthetic quality-progression (a dramatic minor example of the movies' gradual maturing in all areas) of the four versions of *Madame X* (1920, 1929, 1937, 1966).

So in dating these fifty outstanding examples of the Romantic School from 1932 on, I am offering the best Hollywood had to offer in any given area or aspect of Romance, and many are the ways of love, as these variations on the theme attest.

Of course the implicit irony herein is that many "remakes of remakes" represented a regression rather than a progression. While the 1941 *Back Street* proved greatly superior in quality to the 1932 original, the 1961 version was much below the standard of both its predecessors. The 1973 *Lost Horizon* does not compare with the splendidly wrought 1937 picture. The 1941 *Smilin' Through* must take second place to the 1932 masterpiece. The 1962 *The Children's Hour*, despite the fact that it retained the title of the 1934 play, followed its theme more faithfully, and even boasted the same director (William Wyler) did not match in any respect the quality of the 1936 *These Three*. The 1971 *Wuthering Heights* wasn't in the same league with the one of 1939, nor was the 1973 *The Nelson Affair* with the 1941 *That Hamilton Woman*.

On the other side of the ledger, the 1957 *Barretts of Wimpole Street* outclassed the 1934 original, and the 1966 *Madame X* gave a more realistic, moving and psychologically more penetrating insight into the theme (and was more polished technically) than its three predecessors.

Accordingly, we chose the versions that in our view represented the best edition of a well-known story. We strove for variety, and we tried to touch all bases.

The theme of mother love, which however platonic and spiritualized, constitutes one of the most enduring and profound of human romances, is explored in such films as *Stella Dallas*, *To Each His Own* and *Madame X*, and forms a subsidiary, but potent component of others on our list, for instance, *Only Yesterday*, *The Life of Vergie Winters*, *The Old Maid*, *This Love of Ours*.

Unrequited love is depicted in various colorations and shadings in *These Three*, *The Old Maid*, *Lydia*, *Random Harvest*, *A Stolen Life*, *Letter From An Unknown Woman*, *The Heiress*, *Rhapsody*.

Romantic themes enriched by musical backgrounds are represented by *Maytime*, *Intermezzo*, *A Song to Remember*, *Humoresque*, *Song of Love*, *Rhapsody*, *The Loves of Isadora* and *The Music Lovers*.

The "back street syndrome," as the theme of secret triangular love has been humorously dubbed in some quarters, gets a thorough airing from *Back Street* through *The Life of Vergie Winters*, *Only Yesterday*, and some aspects of *The House on 56th Street* and *To Each His Own*.

9

The sorrows of "off-horse" boyhood and the idealistic love of one boy for another are poignantly set forth in *No Greater Glory*. And the "off-horse" adolescent is movingly portrayed in *Tea and Sympathy* in a theme involving a sensitive youth and an older married woman.

Homosexual emotion, concealed or overt, a subject that has come into increasing prominence in recent years, gets attention in *Teorema*, *The Music Lovers*, *Death in Venice* and *A Separate Peace*.

Romance between partners in which age difference plays a role is featured in *All That Heaven Allows*, *The Roman Spring of Mrs. Stone* and *Love and Pain And The Whole Damn Thing*.

People with psychological or physical afflictions who find escape and renewal in romantic love are represented in *The Barretts of Wimpole Street*; *King's Row*; *Now, Voyager*; and *Love and Pain*.

Nor are supernatural aspects of Romance neglected. In *Death Takes a Holiday*, Death takes human form and courts a girl with mystical leanings. In *Smilin' Through* a girl long dead waits for her lover to join her in eternity, and in *Maytime* the sexes are reversed for a reworking of the same basic theme. In *Portrait of Jennie* the spirit of a long-dead girl engages in a supernatural romance with a painter. In *Teorema* a strange young man who may be God, the Devil, Christ or merely the spirit of Truth and Beauty profoundly affects every member of an Italian family. And in *Death in Venice*, a dying composer encounters a charismatic fifteen-year-old who is, among other things, a representation of the Angel of Death. In *The Enchanted Cottage*, Love makes two ugly people beautiful.

Death terminates love stories in *Only Yesterday*, *The House on 56th Street*, *Camille*, *Maytime*, *To Each His Own*, *Letter From an Unknown Woman*, *My Foolish Heart* and *Love Story*.

The degradations and humiliations of aging romantics who resort to gigolos are depicted in *The Roman Spring of Mrs. Stone*. The altruism of unselfish giving is the theme of *The Blue Veil* in which a woman dedicates her life to the care and nurturing of a succession of children, a special variety of Romance that deserves its place here.

Romance portrayed against lavish historical backgrounds: *That Hamilton Woman*, *Marie Antoinette*, *A Song To Remember*, *The Loves of Isadora*. And the Romance of the Free Spirit who defies convention to live by his or her own rules can be examined, as a major or subsidiary theme in many of the above, and especially in *All That Heaven Allows*, *The Loves of Isadora* and *A Song To Remember*.

Houses can be romantic, especially if they are redolent with old associations, as in *The House on 56th Street* and *Enchantment*.

Through these pages parade a host of stars who symbolized romance in its various aspects down through the decades: Bette Davis, loving unrequitedly in *A Stolen Life*, changing from ugly duckling into swan in *Now, Voyager*, eating her heart out with hidden frustrations and tormenting guilts in *The Old Maid*. Merle Oberon, defying convention to dress as a man in *A Song To Remember*, striving to renew acquaintance, and reaffirm mother-love, with a daughter she hasn't seen in years in *This Love of Ours*, for forty years carrying a torch for a man who has long forgotten her in *Lydia*. Margaret Sullavan, who agonizes over a World War I lover who has likewise forgotten he ever knew her, but has left her with an illegitimate son; and who remains faithful for twenty-five years to a man too selfish to divorce his wife (*Only Yesterday* and *Back Street*). Norma Shearer, touching and true as the wraith Moonyean in *Smilin' Through* who waits fifty years for her beloved in death; life-denying and then life-affirming after she meets Robert Browning in *The Barretts of Wimpole Street*; chained to a loveless marriage and loving Tyrone Power hopelessly in *Marie Antoinette*.

Jennifer Jones, conducting a supernatural romance with Joseph Cotten in *Portrait of Jennie*; Dirk Bogarde, obsessed with the mystic teen-ager in *Death in Venice*; Evelyn Venable, who surrenders her being to Death himself in *Death Takes a Holiday*.

Joan Crawford, one of the great romantic screen images, committing suicide in *Humoresque* because she knows Love has only sorrow and disillusion to offer; blackmailing the world because of her scarred face in *A Woman's Face* but eventually redeemed by plastic surgery and requited love. Ann Harding, gracious, patrician, suffering elegantly through *The Life of Vergie Winters*, opposite John Boles, the basically decent guy who found himself a reluctant *homme fatale* in *Back Street* and *Only Yesterday* and the victim of a misfit marriage in *Stella Dallas*.

Barbara Stanwyck, the most romantic and touching of all mother figures as *Stella Dallas*; the widow who brings gossip on herself and almost loses her sons with an ill-advised romance in *My Reputation*. And Garbo the Inimitable, romancing, and romanced by, an ardent Robert Taylor in *Camille*. Ronald Colman, struggling with amnesia in *Random Harvest* while his true love, Greer Garson, stands by patiently. Katharine Hepburn, aspiring to the love of a boy above her class in *Alice Adams*; faithful to a brilliant composer-husband going slowly insane in *Song of Love*.

Houses bring back memories of love long lost to Kay Francis in *The House on 56th Street* and David Niven in *Enchantment*. Ingrid Bergman convinces herself she cannot build happiness on the unhappiness of others as the odd-girl-out in a triangularly romantic *Intermezzo*. Olivier the Demon Lover frightens Oberon the Spiritually Ambivalent into the arms of safe, staid Niven in *Wuthering Heights*, but only for a time; and Ronald Colman again, returning to Shangri-La, the lost paradise of all men's dreams, in *Lost Horizon*.

Ronald Reagan gets his legs cut off in *King's Row* but Ann Sheridan loves him all the more. Elizabeth Taylor learns that mature love involves personal responsibility in *Rhapsody*. And Vanessa Redgrave at forty-nine has one last fling with a handsome stranger and dances a frenzied tango with him before breaking her neck when her scarf is caught in the wheel-spokes of his Bugatti in *The Loves of Isadora*.

Romantics all—but the world loves a lover, at least cinema audiences by the many millions did during the Depression Thirties, when Romance in the Movies offered the ultimate Mass Escape, and during the war-torn and postwar Forties, when Escape was required as never before, and even through the smug Eisenhower Fifties, when God was still in his Heaven and all was right with the world, and Love and Romance were considered legitimate components of the human condition and experience.

And then the 1960s—and the 1970s—when "love" pictures grew few and far between.

The *American College Dictionary* defines "Romance" as "a tale depicting heroic or marvelous achievements, colorful events or scenes, chivalrous devotion; unusual, even supernatural, experiences, or other matters of a kind to appeal to the imagination." The dictionary definition continues: "a made-up story, fanciful or extravagant invention or exaggeration" and concludes with "to indulge in fanciful or extravagant stories."

And what happened to the "romantic," the "supernatural," the "fanciful," the "unusual," to say nothing of "matters of a kind to appeal to the imagination"—during the Dark Sixties?

In a 1973 book, *Where The Wasteland Ends*, Theodore Roszak wrote:

I cannot recall that I have ever heard the word "Romantic" applied approvingly to a contemporary work of art or thought. The adjective, well exercised in abusive criticism, drips contempt or condescension; a diagnosis of emotional indigestion. Moonstruck lovers and Byronic seizures, great cloudy symbols and Faustian ardor no longer appeal to more sophisticated tastes—primarily, I suspect, because few of us, once past adolescence, dare make ourselves as vulnerable as the Romantic sensibility demands. We have not the courage to risk the folly of strong feeling, much less the innocence.

In my 1966 article *Great Romantic Films of the Past*, which bore the subtitle *Why Can't Hollywood Duplicate Them Today?* I put it another way, and it still applies eight years later:

The lines of a famous poem end with the words, "The light of the whole world dies when Love is Done."

And what many observers of today's film scene would like to know is: Has Hollywood Done with Love?

Certainly it has lost the knack for the feelingful and poetically conceived films that once distinguished its output—films that refreshed an audience's emotional insight, films that reaffirmed the spiritual values that—as is too often forgotten in this sex-ridden, dehumanized era—conveyed unmistakable intimations of the deepest of all truths: that Love is the most mystical, and most spiritually revealing, of all the emotions.

Look at today's movies. So many of them convey the idea that Sex is Love, indeed the whole of Love. Our deeper intuitions teach us that Sex is only a part of Love. If one loves without exaltation, without warmth, without feeling, then one is only *sexually* enthralled. Yet Sex today is deified, along with its distant relation Sadism, and its cousins of the Masochist family, as if they were the be-all and end-all of human relationships.

It wasn't like that in the old days. The days when people didn't regard Love as "corny" and Sentiment as "mawkish" and Loyalty and Devotion as "icky." We live in an age that is ashamed of Emotion as if it were a weakness, or an embarrassing flaw of character. And in such distortions lies the basic negation of our time. For the day that Love—on-screen and off—became "old-fashioned" was the day that the Darkness of the Heart came to reign.

Now, in 1974, there are faint signs of Spring amidst the Snows of Anomie, Spiritual Depletion and the chronic substitution of words like "communication" for words like "love."

We hear of lectures on "The Return of Romanticism." It seems to be gradually coming back into our literature. Stage drama and musical comedies rehash nostalgic love stories. And the films, which slowly began to get back on their humanistic feet after wallowing throughout the Sixties in nihilistic, life-denying, love-denying brutishness and sex-obsessiveness, to say nothing of endless varieties of hate and violence, are coming out with films that grow more and more romantic. True, the writers of the 1970s are still frightened of full-strength emotion, and the pictures often seem choked-up, self-conscious, crudely allusive when they should be honestly emotional. But beginning with *Love Story* in 1970 (a flawed film but nonetheless one that set the stage for the return of Romance in the Movies) and continuing through *Death in Venice* and *Love and Pain and The Whole Damn Thing* and others, there is a definite trend toward the reenthronement of the Romantic Sensibility in a medium it helped to make great, and which again, hopefully, it will rescue from the Dark Ages of Lovelessness to which it has for years been condemned.

The
Great
Romantic
Films

Smilin'
Through

Metro-
Goldwyn-
Mayer

1932

CREDITS: Directed by Sidney Franklin. Screenplay and Adaptation by Ernest Vajda and James Bernard Fagan. Based on the play by Jane Cowl and Jane Murfin. Photographed by Lee Garmes. Edited by Margaret Booth.

OPENED at the Capitol Theatre, New York, October 14, 1932. Running time: 96 minutes.

CAST: Norma Shearer (Moonyean Clare-Kathleen Clare); Leslie Howard (John Carteret); Fredric March (Jeremy Wayne-Kenneth Wayne); O. P. Heggie (Doctor Owen); Ralph Forbes (Willie Ainley); Beryl Mercer (Mrs. Crouch); David Torrence (gardener); Margaret Seddon (Ellen); Forrester Harvey (orderly); Cora Sue Collins (young Kathleen).

Norma Shearer and Leslie Howard

One of the great romances on both stage and screen, *Smilin' Through* retains its enduring appeal. The secret of its charm and power, undiminished through the decades, lies in its perfect fusion of the romantic and the supernatural, with a story so haunting and emotional as to cast a spell over viewers of any era. Even today, when respect for the mystique of the supernatural has reached a relatively low ebb, *Smilin' Through* in revival affects even the spiritually alienated young of the 1970s. Its sincerity is irresistible, its depth unquestioned, its purity of spirit an enchantment in itself.

It first appeared as a well-loved Broadway play coauthored by Jane Cowl and Jane Murfin, and coming as it did in the wake of World War I, its philosophical approach and emotional depth kept theatre audiences enthralled. After its stage triumph, it was inevitable that it would find its way into the silent films, and in 1922 Norma Talmadge starred in a picture version that, while creditable for its time, takes distinct second place to the handsome, well-mounted 1932 version starring Norma Shearer, Leslie Howard and Fredric March.

With this, its third incarnation, *Smilin' Through* was transposed to the sound medium at exactly the right moment. Sound had arrived full force by 1929—and by 1932 the talented artisans and technicians who helped raise the art of film to its highest level were in complete command of their medium. A careful look at the 1932 product of the Hollywood studios reveals that the crudities of the early talkies had been planed away. The Shearer-March-Howard version of *Smilin' Through* represented the fullest expression of many talents. Moreover, it was a subject that demanded apposite mood music, sensitive direction, delicate photographic nuances, polished acting—of the kind silent films could not provide in such depth and coloration.

The radiant Miss Shearer was in top form in this tragic tale of a love frustrated through many years, destined for fruition only in eternity. Miss Shearer was ably complemented by Howard's and March's skillful performances. Sidney Franklin, one of the most discerning of directors, did wonders with the overall ambience, and Lee Garmes's photography was richly inventive and technically resourceful, especially in the supernatural scenes.

The third and final film version of *Smilin' Through* was made in 1941 with Jeanette MacDonald in the Shearer role, and Brian Aherne and Gene Raymond (Miss MacDonald's husband) in the Howard and March roles respectively. Somehow it lacked the grace, spontaneity and supernatural power of the 1932 version and the result took on the look of a thrice-told tale—four times told, if one counts the stage version. Part of the trouble lay with the scoring. (By the 1940s MGM films tended, for some strange reason, to overdo the mood music to the point of drowning out the dialogue in some instances.) In addition, the action tended to stop cold in order to sandwich in songs for Miss Mac-

Norma Shearer

Fredric March and Norma Shearer

March flees the country, and Howard grieves down through the years.

Some thirty years after the tragedy, Shearer's niece Kathleen (also played by Shearer) comes to live with Howard after her parents are drowned. A genuine father-daughter attachment grows between them. One day the niece, totally ignorant of the old tragedy, takes refuge from a storm in the decaying old house that Jeremy Wayne had left exactly as it was on the day of the shooting; amidst the dust and cobwebs she and her escort Willie Ainley (Ralph Forbes) find an overturned chair, a wine carafe, an 1868 newspaper—and, even after fifty years, a lingering sense of something terrible that had happened in that room. When later she reports her adventure to her aged uncle, he flies into a rage. During her visit to the empty old house she had encountered Wayne's son Kenneth (March in a dual role) and an instant attraction sparks between them. Howard bitterly demands that she not see him again, and finally reveals to her the details of his ancient sorrow. Pity for her uncle triumphs over her growing love for March, and she agrees.

March goes to war, and comes back wounded. The wraith of Moonyean, who has appeared to Howard through the years whenever he expresses a need of her spiritual consolation, informs him that there will be no eternal reunion for them unless he forgives and forgets, and allows his niece to marry Wayne's son. Sensitive at last to Kathleen's torment, he sends her to her love, whereupon Moonyean's wraith again appears to tell her patient lover that his fifty years of waiting are over at last and that they belong to each other forever now. Howard rises, once more young and handsome, from the old man who has died, and he and Shearer get into a coach surrounded by a wedding party. On their way down the lane they pass the present-day couple returning to the house, and smile on them fondly.

The theme song, "Smilin' Through," became an instant hit, and its haunting melody is still familiar.

Smilin' Through belongs to an era that was somehow more spiritually healthy—a time when Death was accepted in the midst of Life. The fear of Death, the constant efforts to stave it off, or ignore its inevitability, that characterizes more current thinking, was in those days sublimated and transmuted into a romanticization of what is after all a natural human phenomenon. Death was often regarded as a friend, with this life and its appurtenances *not* regarded as the Be-All and End-All. Through that time of soul and spirit, the 1930s, other highly romantic films (see *Death Takes a Holiday, Maytime, Wuthering Heights*) played on the same principle. They suggest to the society of the 1970s that the shifting attitudes toward Death have introduced something craven, mean and negative, something myopic, for what once flourished on the human scene as a beautiful and fulfilling sublimatory instinct.

Donald and somehow these interpolations jarred with the fragile original conception. The director, Frank Borzage, was sensitive and perceptive (see the text for *No Greater Glory*) and it does not detract from his gifts to state that in 1941 *Smilin' Through* was a tale told once too often.

The story deals with the tragic Moonyean Clare (Shearer) who in the England of 1868 falls in love with country squire John Carteret (Leslie Howard). She is coveted by the half-crazed, heavy-drinking Jeremy Wayne (Fredric March) and on the day of her wedding to Howard he follows them to the church and kills Miss Shearer with a bullet meant for her groom. As she dies in Howard's arms, surrounded by the grieving wedding guests, she promises that she will always be near him, and that in the fullness of time they will be forever united.

O. P. Heggie, Leslie Howard and Norma Shearer

Leslie Howard and Norma Shearer

Only
Yesterday

Universal

1933

CREDITS: Directed by John M. Stahl. Adapted by Arthur Richman and George O'Neill. Story suggested from the book "Only Yesterday" by Frederick Lewis Allen. Dialogue by William Hurlburt. Photographed by Merrit Gerstad.

OPENED at Radio City Music Hall, New York, November 9, 1933. Running time: 105 minutes.

CAST: Margaret Sullavan (Mary Lane); John Boles (James Emerson); Jimmy Butler (Jim Jr.); Billie Burke (Julia Warren); Reginald Denny (Bob); Edna May Oliver (Leona); Benita Hume (Phyllis Emerson); George Meeker (Dave Reynolds); June Clyde (Deborah); Oscar Apfel (Mr. Lane); Jane Darwell (Mrs. Lane); Tom Conlon (Bob Lane); Burton Churchill (Goodheart); Onslow Stevens (Barnard); Franklin Pangborn (Tom); Walter Catlett (Barnes); Noel Francis (Letitia); Bramwell Fletcher (Scott Hughes); Barry Norton (Jerry); Arthur Hoyt (Burton); Natalie Moorhead (Lucy); Joyce Compton (Margot); Betty Blythe (Mrs. Vincent); Grady Sutton (Charlie Smith); Ruth Clifford (Eleanor); Dorothy Grainger (Sally); Geneva Mitchell (Patty); Dorothy Christy (Rena); and Huntley Gordon, Herbert Corthell, Richard Tucker, Craufurd Kent, Marie Prevost, Vivien Oakland, Bert Roach, Julia Faye, Robert Ellis, Leo White, Cissy Fitzgerald.

Jimmy Butler and John Boles

Margaret Sullavan and Billie Burke

Only Yesterday, even by 1933 standards, did not contain the freshest of material—in fact, it was a hodgepodge of banalities, but it had the fresh, appealing and unique radiance of Margaret Sullavan in her first screen performance; a down-to-earth, human approach; the sure, seasoned, painstaking direction of John M. Stahl (*Back Street*) who was an old hand at "women's picture" material, and situations and dialogue that were often tender, touching and true.

A standard romantic "special" of the kind so popular in the early 1930s, it was redolent of many other films that had gone before, including such disparate items as *The Big Parade*, *The White Sister*, *Madame X*, *The Sin of Madelon Claudet* and the aforementioned *Back Street*, which had appeared only the year before. But between them, Miss Sullavan, Mr. Stahl, the reliable John Boles, the inventive screenwriters and an engaging new child actor named Jimmy Butler (also making his film debut) managed to turn *Only Yesterday* into a 1933 smash of major proportions.

Miss Sullavan in this made one of the most impressive screen debuts of any major star, with the 1933 critics praising her fresh, if muted, beauty and her intelligence and radiance as Mary Lane, the girl who loves not wisely but too pridefully. The story opens in 1929, with broker Jim Emerson (Boles) losing all his money in the crash and going home to his study to commit suicide, thus emulating many of his unlucky Wall Street confreres on Black Tuesday. But before raising the gun to his head, he sees a letter on his desk and proceeds to read it. The letter changes his life and gives him fresh hope for the future despite his reduced circumstances. Written by Miss Sullavan, the missive traces the twelve years during which she has loved him hopelessly from a distance.

The story begins in 1917 when Boles, a young lieutenant in a Southern training camp during World War I, meets Virginia belle Sullavan at a dance. They fall in love, know one fulfilling night together, and then he goes to France. The Boles character is portrayed as that of an honorable, decent and sin-

Margaret Sullavan and John Boles

Billie Burke and Margaret Sullavan

cere young man not usually given to philandering. This enhances the poignancy of the subsequent events. Miss Sullavan finds herself pregnant, goes to New York to stay with an understanding aunt, Billie Burke, and is delivered there of Boles's child. When the War ends, and the victorious soldiers parade up Fifth Avenue, Miss Sullavan goes to find her love. Though he has not written her, she believes implicitly that he is faithful to her as she is to him, that he remembers, and still loves her. She confronts him amidst a group of his friends after the parade, but the vacant, politely uncomprehending stare he gives her forces her to realize he has completely erased the memory of her from his mind. Shattered, she withdraws, and pride prevents her from enlightening him further.

Later she reads of his marriage in a newspaper, and puts her hopes permanently aside. Successful in business, Sullavan raises their son, Jimmy Butler, into a fine boy of ten, a military school cadet. On a New Year's Eve ten years after the War, she and Boles meet again at a party. She has never ceased to love him, and with a rueful sadness she grants him still another night of love, though he does not realize she is the girl he once loved briefly in Virginia, nor does she choose to tell him. The next morning she goes away and he regards the interlude as a "one-night stand" and proceeds once more to forget all about her. But her heart is weak, and when she realizes she is dying, she writes, telling him of their son. Boles goes to her home to find she has died, but the boy is there, grieving in his military school uniform. In a moving final scene, Boles reveals to him that he is his father.

Jimmy Butler and Margaret Sullavan

Margaret Sullavan

That is the sum total of the plot, but it is redeemed by the fine acting and its 105 minutes (quite long for a 1933 drama) go by quickly thanks to Stahl's pacing and professionalism. John Boles by 1933 had really hit his stride as the man-who-proves-fatal-to-women, the first version of *Back Street* (1932) opposite Irene Dunne having set the style and tone of many subsequent Boles performances. A handsome, gentlemanly fellow who had begun as a singer (*Rio Rita* et al.), Boles in retrospect was a better actor than he was credited as being at the time (for instance in the 1936 *Craig's Wife*) and in *Only Yesterday* he portrayed an attractive character attractively. Miss Sullavan, who had won her acting spurs on the New York stage after thorough stock training, proved a revelation in her screen debut, and immediately became a major star. A natural, unassuming performer, she was a gifted actress and *Only Yesterday* got her off to the right Hollywood start.

Amid a host of talented character performers in support, Billie Burke and Reginald Denny provided well-bred comedy relief, as in a scene where Miss Burke (an inimitable character performer) sings off-key to husband Denny's piano accompaniment. *Only Yesterday* also catapulted the winning child actor Jimmy Butler into prominence and led him directly into leading roles in such as Frank Borzage's *No Greater Glory* the following year. Jimmy Butler was to die a sad early death, his original promise unfulfilled (see text for *No Greater Glory*) but his later performances of the 1930s keep his memory alive.

Only Yesterday has its share of touching scenes —Sullavan's chagrined sorrow when Boles fails to recognize her at the Fifth Avenue parade; their belated reunion ten years later under ironic circumstances; Boles's claiming of his son. Some 1933 critics objected to the improbability of Boles's faulty memory (the screenwriters didn't even bother to shore up its credibility via a World War I "shell-shock" gimmick or something similar), but on the whole they elected for "suspension of disbelief" in the face of the strong emotional values implicit in the story's handling.

A romantic film of the deepest dye, 1933-vintage, *Only Yesterday* still stirs fond memories in the post-fifty set and commands interest in film buffs viewing it today. The title was taken from Frederick Lewis Allen's survey of the 1918–33 period; otherwise the scholarly Allen commentary on a significant American era has nothing to do with the essentially intimate screen romance. Some of the atmosphere of the period, however, was cleverly worked in via contemporary references and montages.

John Boles and Margaret Sullavan

The
House

on
56th
Street

Warner
Bros.

1933

CREDITS: Directed by Robert Florey. Screenplay by Austin Parker and Sheridan Gibney. Based on the novel by Joseph Stanley. Photographed by Ernest Haller. Edited by Bud Bretherton.

OPENED at the Hollywood Theatre, New York, December 1, 1933. Running time: 69 minutes.

CAST: Kay Francis (Peggy); Ricardo Cortez (Blaine); Gene Raymond (Monte Van Tyle); John Halliday (Fiske); Margaret Lindsay (Eleanor); Frank McHugh (Hunt); Sheila Terry (Dolly); William Boyd (Bonelli); Hardie Albright (Henry); Philip Faversham (Gordon); Nella Walker (Mrs. Van Tyle).

Kay Francis and Gene Raymond

William Boyd, Ricardo Cortez and Kay Francis

The House on 56th Street is not only a touching, nostalgic love story—it is also the romance of a New York house. In a sense it can be described as a sociological romance, for it reflects the profound social and environmental changes in America from 1905 to 1933. The film also contains Kay Francis's finest performance, in the type of role that made her a household name in the 1930s.

The film holds up well in revival, and seems solidly set in the periods that it describes. There is a built-in poignancy in the depiction of the gradual downhill course of a once-elegant town house on New York's East 56th Street near Park Avenue—a residence that once in 1905 had sheltered the flower of the aristocracy—the young man (Gene Raymond) whom Miss Francis loves and loses—and which by 1933 has become a gambling establishment run by hoodlums who exploit the well-heeled and the unwary. Miss Francis keeps expertly abreast of the story line's downward trend, running the gamut from the bright hopefulness of a young marriage to the man she loves to the embittering realities of an aging woman buffeted by fate and forced to relive sad memories in the once-radiant, now-grim setting where she had known a short-lived happiness long before. The picture is a unique one of its kind; and the theme is sufficiently unusual to have known

few duplications, or even approximations of theme, among the thousands of screenplays Hollywood has turned out.

Director Robert Florey complemented the screenwriters by suffusing the film with tender nostalgia and a telling sense of what the years and the vicissitudes of living, as well as the contrarinesses of fate, can do to one human sprit. Miss Francis in the opening scenes is a New York chorus girl, 1905 vintage, who deserts her wealthy aging lover, John Halliday, for true love, handsome Knickerbocker scion Gene Raymond. He takes her to their new home, a brownstone mansion on East 56th Street, and their idyllic felicity is played out for a few years, which see the arrival of a baby daughter. On the first occasion the young bride and groom had visited the mansion, Raymond had pointed out to her a small Florentine medallion on the fireplace mantel—the face of a small boy—and tells her it is a key symbol of their happiness and that they will live and love in that room and in that house "forever."

"Forever" turns out to be all too brief, for jilted swain Halliday insists on winning back Miss Francis, wife and mother though she be, and she indiscreetly visits his apartment to bring him to his senses. The disgruntled and disappointed Halliday

Kay Francis and William Boyd

threatens suicide and in the struggle for his gun, it goes off and he falls dead. As such 1933-style romances would have it, Miss Francis is accused of the murder, gets off with manslaughter, and languishes for twenty years in prison. Her one great love, her young husband, continues to believe in her innocence but dies in France in World War I. in 1925 she emerges from prison, a still-handsome but sadly benumbed woman in her forties. Her husband's family settle a sum of money on her and tell her to stay away from her now-grown daughter, whom she hasn't seen since babyhood.

The quality of life in New York and the world has changed greatly in those twenty years; the pace has quickened immeasurably; it is no longer the era of Floradora sextets, proud and elegant East Side mansions and hansom cabs. Now speakeasies and gambling dens flourish. On an ocean trip, Francis meets cardsharp Ricardo Cortez, and puts to good use the adept ease with cards she had learned from her gambler father. Soon she and her new friend are teaming up, with considerable success, and after fleecing rich Europeans and transcontinental travelers, they return to New York. Cortez informs her

that he has won for them a gambling concession in a speakeasy on East 56th Street—and nostalgic consternation is visible in Miss Francis's face when she steps out of the taxi—to face her old home. She goes into the mansion, now so changed, yet containing many of the old fixtures and wainscoting—and there is the nursery, and the Florentine fireplace medallion her one-true-love-long-gone had cherished with her. Presently she is dealing blackjack in these forlorn surroundings, with the past her constant specter.

To the gambling den comes Francis's daughter, Margaret Lindsay, who has inherited her forebears' gambling fever, and one night when she loses heavily and Cortez threatens to tell her family and fiancé, who has demanded she stop gambling, the daughter shoots and kills him in defensive panic. Miss Francis, her mother-love in the ascendant, tries to assume the onus of the killing, but gambling boss William Boyd covers up for her on condition she remain in his employ in that house "forever." In a moving final fadeout, Miss Francis goes to the fireplace, looks at the Florentine medallion with its boyish, innocent young face, and quietly repeats, "Forever. . . ."

The House on 56th Street is replete with poignant keynote scenes—the shot where she looks up, after twenty years, at the house where all her lost happiness is buried; her first meeting with her daughter, now grown, who is unaware that the sad-eyed, sleek, chicly gowned woman is her mother; her cynical, hard-eyed stance and gestures that conceal a heart long broken but now freshly bleeding, as she deals expert blackjack in what was once her child's nursery.

The period art work is excellent and the photography respectfully detailed, as the house changes and alters—we see the exterior in bright new splendor, the boarding-up of the windows after the tragedy, the slight accumulation of grime on its brownstone front after the years bring back to its bosom the principal actor in that long-gone time of grace. Truly the romance of a house, *The House on 56th Street* is also the romance of love won, cherished briefly, then lost forever; dreams dashed, motherhood thwarted, with the cruelties of time and change borne in on a sensitive, responsive, life-loving woman who for all her worldliness and cynicism is essentially an affirmative, introspective soul forced by Fate into a buried life where she becomes what her memories are.

Originally slated as a Ruth Chatterton vehicle (Chatterton and Francis were Warners' top feminine stars before Bette Davis's full-fledged debut in the later 30s), the film does full credit to the distinctive talents of Kay Francis, one of the more underrated stars of her era. A handsome, poised woman with wonderful large dark eyes, considerable technical resource as an actress, a compelling voice with a distinctive speech trait (Bogart had his lisp and Francis had her r's pronounced as w's), Miss Francis made an ideal "woman's picture" heroine, portraying the many ways of love with an eloquent sincerity and cool authority. *The House on 56th Street* is not only the perfect Kay Francis vehicle—it is in its own right a touching nostalgic romance that haunts the memory. The author saw it when he was ten years old—also in several revivals—yet the impression made by certain scenes is still fresh in mind after forty years. What better test of a film than that?

Margaret Lindsay and Kay Francis

Death Takes a Holiday

Paramount

1934

CREDITS: Directed by Michell Leisen. Screenplay by Maxwell Anderson and Gladys Lehman. Based on a play by Alberto Casella. Photographed by Charles Lang. Art Direction by Hans Dreier and Ernst Figte.

OPENED at the Paramount Theatre, New York, February 23, 1934. Running time: 79 minutes.

CAST: Fredric March (Prince Sirki); Evelyn Venable (Grazia); Sir Guy Standing (Duke Lambert); Katherine Alexander (Alda); Gail Patrick (Rhoda); Helen Westley (Stephanie); Kathleen Howard (Princess Maria); Kent Taylor (Corrado); Henry Travers (Baron Cesarea); G. P. Huntley, Jr. (Eric); Otto Hoffman, (Fedele); Edward Van Sloan (Doctor Valle); Hector Sarno (Pietro); Frank Yaconelli (Vendor); Anna De Linsky (Maid).

The Hollywood preoccupation with Death as a glamorous symbol continued with Fredric March's excellent *Death Takes a Holiday*, one of the unusual and compelling film concoctions of 1934. Not only did it present Mr. March, a recent Academy Award winner for *Dr. Jekyll and Mr. Hyde* (1931), with one of his more glamorous screen incarnations, it also boasted top production values—eerie, fascinating music, handsome mounting, sterling acting performances from the entire cast, and a philosophical and to say the least, unique, approach to Death that was quite revolutionary for its time.

Death Takes a Holiday, moreover, qualifies eminently as a romantic film in that it suggests, and quite eloquently, that the perfection of love is to be found in eternal verities and cosmic spiritual commitments rather than in the frailties and inconsistencies of human attachment, with all their temporal limitations and spiritual imperfections.

This film also highlighted a humanistic legend that has flourished for centuries, the symbol of Death in the form of a handsome young man, an image that has appeared in films and theatre frequently since 1934 (*The Milk Train Doesn't Stop*

Kathleen Howard and Fredric March

*Evelyn Venable
and Fredric March*

Fredric March, Evelyn Venable, Kent Taylor, Kathleen Howard and Sir Guy Standing.

Fredric March and Sir Guy Standing.

Here Any More, The Sandbox, Teorema, Death in Venice, et al.).

Based on a play by Alberto Casella in which Philip Merivale had made a hit, the plot relates how Death made a decision to assume human form in order to learn firsthand about the world of human beings and the fears and misconceptions formed around and about him. He takes on the appearance of a handsome young nobleman, Prince Sirki, and persuades an Italian aristocrat, Sir Guy Standing, to put him up for three days as a member of an exclusive house party. Despite his fearful and reluctant host's trepidations, all goes very well. Several of the female guests are attracted to Prince Sirki, but when one of them pushes her suit too far, he feels obliged to reveal something of his true self (he asks her to stare deep into his eyes) and she withdraws in horror. The well-written script is sometimes amusing; to an aged guest the Prince expresses his wonderment that they had not met before, while in the outside world men leap from heights and walk away unscathed; horrible fires spare their victims and wilted flowers regain their bloom.

With the news full of miraculous escapes from sure fatalities, the guests wonder at Death's strange withdrawal from human affairs, sometimes expressing their puzzlement in terms the prince finds insulting. Meanwhile Sirki, charming, handsome, if a bit strange, continues to throw out verbal ironies. Grazia (Evelyn Venable) is an idealistic girl who is drawn to Sirki and he to her. He finds her different from the others, less worldly, more idealistic and pure-spirited, and she is not only not afraid of him but seems somehow akin in essence. When the Prince tests her by revealing himself as an ominous shade, she seems even more attracted to him, and with the love that has blossomed between them proving mutual, the Prince decides to take her off with him, since his three-day furlough is drawing to an end.

Despite her family's grief, she goes with him, his cloak wrapped around her, for in Death alone has she found, in its ultimate fulfillment, the love for which she has always longed.

The picture holds up very well even after forty years. The obvious care put into every aspect of its production, the fine camera work by Charles Lang, the haunting theme song, Mitchell Leisen's sensitive direction, all stand redeemed by time. True artistry never dates.

Evelyn Venable was affecting, at times even ethereal, as Grazia, and this unique young actress's subsequent Hollywood course seems, in retrospect, a puzzlement (she was soon languishing in small supporting roles in films like *Alice Adams*) as she offered an image that was original and distinctive. Sir Guy Standing as the half-mesmerized, half-terrified nobleman host was also excellent, as he was in many films of this period, as were such supporting players as Henry Travers, Katherine Alexander and

Evelyn Venable and Kent Taylor

Kent Taylor. And March was an arresting figure in monocle, white dinner jacket and foreign accent—a glamorous, talented star in a role superior to many he was handed at the time.

Evelyn Venable and Fredric March

CREDITS: Directed by Frank Borzage. Screenplay by Jo Swerling. Adapted from the novel, "The Paul Street Boys" by Ferenc Molnar. Photographed by Joseph August. Louis Borzage, Assistant Director.

OPENED at the Roxy Theatre, New York, May 4, 1934. Running time: 78 minutes.

CAST: George Breakston (Nemecsek); Jimmy Butler (Boka); Jackie Searl (Gereb); Frankie Darro (Feri Ats); Donald Haines (Csonakos); Rolf Ernest (Ferdie Pasztor); Julius Molnar (Henry Pasztor); Wesley Giraud (Kolnay); Beaudine Anderson (Csele); Bruce Line (Richter); Samuel Hinds (Gereb's Father); Christian Rub (Watchman); Ralph Morgan (Father); Lois Wilson (Mother); Egon Brecher (Racz); Frank Reicher (Doctor); Tom Ricketts (Janitor).

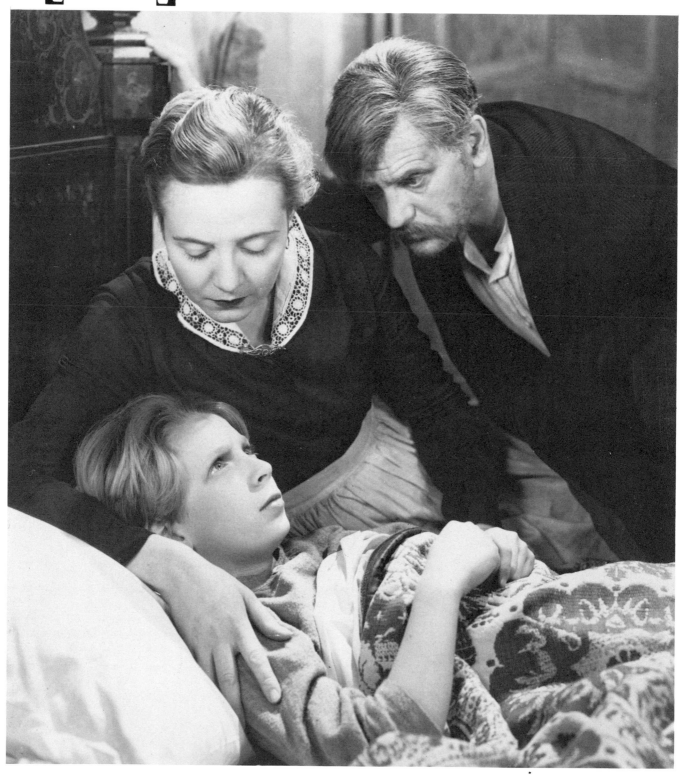

George Breakston, Lois Wilson and Ralph Morgan

his sophisticated plays, pieces that made him world-famous, such as *Liliom, The Guardsman, The Play's The Thing, The Red Mill, The Swan.* His admirers insist that the real Ferenc Molnar is buried in *The Paul Street Boys,* that it is a deeply felt, fully realized evocation of his childhood and his youthful aspirations. Certainly the novel was written with such sensitivity and understanding as to astonish aficionados of the playwright's later work. And the miracle of both book and film is that we, like Molnar, find so much of our own buried life in it, and cherish it on each viewing as its author cherished it in its conception.

No Greater Glory delves, as have few films before or since, into the world of childhood, which so many look back on as their happiest period, and shows that for many a sensitive youngster, it was a time of deep introspection.

Young Breakston's Nemecsek tags after a gang of boys who wear uniforms and run their lumberyard playground like a military post. Heading the gang is Boka (Jimmy Butler), a handsome, stalwart little fellow who is idolized by Nemecsek and whose approval he constantly seeks. But Nemecsek is an outcast; he is frail and delicate, inept at the assorted skills the others regard as mandatory. The impatient, barely tolerant Boka is forever consigning him to his black book for shortcomings and minor ineptitudes. The only "private" in an army of "officers," Nemecsek is held in contempt and condescension for

The childhood sorrows of a lonely misfit have long been the legitimate subject for romantic fiction, and Frank Borzage's sensitively directed film version of the Hungarian writer Ferenc Molnar's novel, *The Paul Street Boys,* retitled *No Greater Glory* for the screen, is a work of surpassing tenderness, taking us into the poignant inner world of an eleven-year-old boy forced into isolation by a delicate constitution.

As played by George Breakston, one of the more gifted of the child actors who flourished in the Hollywood of the Thirties, Nemecsek emerges as an enduring character. I first saw *No Greater Glory* in the Capitol Theatre in Lynn, Massachusetts in 1934 when I was myself eleven, and for forty years it has remained, in retrospect, a profound and moving experience. Seen on TV in recent years, the film retains for me every iota of its original beauty. It is always interesting to see in childhood a film at the time it was made, and then decades later to view it again in revival, and it is surprising how often the original impression is sustained, indeed enhanced. In 1934 as a boy, feeling and sharing in my then day-to-day experience much of what went on in that film, I beheld it from a world very different from today's —a world where romance, sentiment, honest idealism were accepted as a matter of course. Yet when I saw it again, recently, my impression of it remained the same.

The novel on which it was based, *The Paul Street Boys,* was said to be Ferenc Molnar's favorite work. Molnar's reputation, of course, was based on

Jimmy Butler, Jackie Searl, George Breakston and Donald Haines holding the Ferenc Molnar novel, The Paul Street Boys, *on which the film was based*

his failure to "cope" in physical and coordinational terms, although in the actualities of his soul he is a martyr and visionary in the making, the one pure spirit of the lot.

Boka, the legendary personification of the Perfect Friend and Ideal Comrade, seems hopelessly removed from his worshipper Nemecsek—and Nemecsek's efforts to draw close to him, and to win the approval and friendship of the other boys, brings him, in time, not the healing consolations of palship for which he longs, but rather suffering, illness and death. Yet in the end he dies happy, for his idolized Boka, aware finally of Nemecsek's inwardly heroic and sterling qualities, awards him his officer's cap at a bedside visit—and later, when Death overtakes Nemecsek, he feels, in his hard-won, dearly achieved closeness to Boka and his gang, the fulfillment and peace for which he has always longed.

The film is also an allegorical preachment against War—the ironic futility of the Paul Street Boys' struggle against the rival gang of older, tougher guys, the Red Shirts, being borne out when after their victory their lumberyard "fortress" is dredged up for a housing development. Frank Borzage, with the able assistance of screenwriter Jo Swerling, ably depicts Nemecsek's determined battle for acceptance. When the boys' flag is stolen he goes to the enemy stronghold to boldly reclaim it. The tough gang run by Frankie Darro ducks him again and again in cold water, bringing on pneumonia, yet so spiritually hardy is his persistence that he wins even their respect. His parents, Lois Wilson and Ralph Morgan, are poor and hardworking, and cannot attend him constantly after he lies ill—and when he hears that his beloved Boka and his "officers" are about to engage in a final, no-holds-barred battle with the Darro ruffians, he rises from his sickbed to fight among them. In a moving scene, Lois Wilson carries her dead son from the "battleground" with the tearful Jimmy Butler and his aides close behind. Boka has learned, too late, that the boy he had long held in contempt for his lack of the surface qualities that charm the young, is the most loving and loyal friend he ever had.

No Greater Glory won considerable respect from the 1934 critics, and reminded 1934 audiences that the intense attachments of boyhood had much emotional validity. And in Jimmy Butler, handsome, stalwart, the screen gave us the personification of every boy's ideal pal, the transcendent image ex-

George Breakston, Lois Wilson and Jimmy Butler

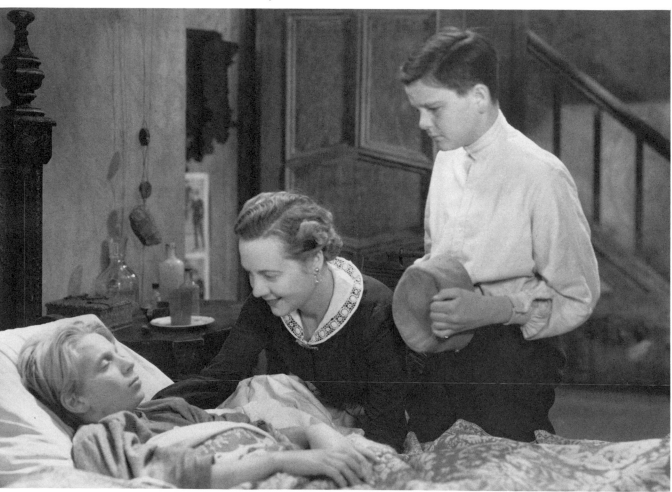

Jimmy Butler (foreground, second left) and his "officers"

tolled by the philosopher Santayana—clean, wholesome, good, well-intentioned.

Jimmy Butler's presence in what was essentially an antiwar drama had its ironic aspects, for this fine young actor was to die, age twenty-four, on February 18, 1945, killed in action in France as an artillery private in World War II. He left a widow, former Horace Heidt band vocalist Jean Fahrney, and two infant sons. After his smash debut as Margaret Sullavan's son in *Only Yesterday*, he was conspicuously cast in such Thirties films as *Manhattan Melodrama, Naval Academy, Nurse Edith Cavell, Romance in Manhattan* and *Mrs. Wiggs of*

the Cabbage Patch, and had he returned from World War II he might have developed an estimable adult acting career. But it was not to be.

But still Jimmy Butler lives, in fading prints of *No Greater Glory*, the prince of many a forlorn boy's dream, the lost ideal of childhood, a romantic image of strengthful goodness, beauty and truth. In creating, and fleshing-out Boka, the character he enacted, Molnar, Borzage and Swerling invested it, and him, with their finest intuitions. The result still shows on the screen, though *No Greater Glory* is now forty years old, and their young hero has been nearly 30 years in his premature grave.

Advertising poster for No Greater Glory

The Life of Vergie Winters

RKO-Radio

1934

CREDITS: Directed by Alfred Santell. Produced by Pandro S. Berman. Adapted by Jane Murfin from the novel, *A Good Woman* by Louis Bromfield. Photographed by Lucien Andriot. Music by Max Steiner.

OPENED at Radio City Music Hall, New York, June 14, 1934. Running time: 75 minutes.

CAST: Ann Harding (Vergie Winters); John Boles (John Shadwell); Helen Vinson (Laura Shadwell); Joan (Betty Furness); Frank Albertson (Ranny Truesdale); Creighton Chaney (Hugo McQueen); Sara Haden (Winnie Belle); Molly O'Day (Sadie); Ben Alexander (Barry Preston); Donald Crisp (Mike Davey); Josephine Whittell (Madame Claire); Wcslcy Barry (Herbert Somerby).

The original, 1932 version of *Back Street* had set off a wave of "illicit" romance in the movies of the mid-Thirties. *The Life of Vergie Winters* was a prime example of the genre.

Directed by Alfred Santell with a knowing eye, handsomely photographed by Lucien Andriot and replete with Max Steiner music that considerably enhanced the sorrow-laden ambience (Steiner even in his pre-Warner period was notably rescuing mediocre movies with his evocative melodies), *The Life of Vergie Winters* proved just the ticket for millions of women, young, middleaged, and old for that matter, who had cultivated an addiction to watching Ann Harding, one of the Thirties Queens of Women's Pictures, suffer in that glamorous style for which she had become noted.

To assure that Miss Harding suffered in first-rate company, RKO put John Boles opposite her. Mr. Boles, who had selfishly kept Irene Dunne in the Back Street, and who had thoughtlessly sired a child by Margaret Sullavan in *Only Yesterday* without even remembering her or knowing of his paternity until the boy was half-grown, did his 1934 *homme fatal* stint by condemning Miss Harding to twenty years of stultifying smalltown existence while he climbed to political eminence.

As is usual in such stories, there is an illegitimate child somewhere in the picture. It seems, ladies, that Mr. Boles in 1910 had been in love with Miss Harding, but due to the manipulative chicanery of relatives, he found himself married instead to Miss Helen Vinson (Gail Patrick's rival in the 1930s for the title of Bitch you Love to Hate.) Later, he and Miss Vinson adopt his and Miss Harding's love-child, and Miss Harding nobly forbids him to divorce his wife because of the possible effects on his political career. Years pass while Miss Harding languishes in her dress shop and Mr. Boles and Miss Vinson peregrinate grandly between Washington and home base. It seems then that Mr. Boles, having waited an unconscionably long time by anyone's standards, insists on divorcing Miss Vinson and taking up full-time with Miss Harding, whom he has been seeing surreptitiously all those years, but that mean Miss Vinson will have none of it, follows Boles to his inamorata's home and shoots him dead.

Miss Harding, for reasons that remain obscure, nobly takes the blame for the shooting and off she goes to prison (the film opens with her languishing in the town jail while her lover's funeral procession goes up the main street outside). But later, as in all good romances of this vintage, she is liberated by Miss Vinson's deathbed confession and her now-grown daughter, Betty Furness, who has Learned All, comes to take her true mother home. Fadeout to Max Steiner's music.

Allowing for the fact that no cheerful prognostication seems possible for the awkward domestic

Josephine Whittell (left) and Ann Harding

John Boles and Betty Furness

Ann Harding and John Boles

Ann Harding, left

accommodation this brings about, what with Miss Furness having a young man (Frank Albertson) in tow who, was not likely to relish this peculiar brand of mother-in-law trouble, as well as for other glaring inconsistencies of motivation and interrelationship, *The Life of Vergie Winters* works better than one would think, especially if the viewer—especially the 1974 viewer—suspends disbelief. There is that afore-

John Boles and Ann Harding

Ann Harding, right

mentioned Steiner score that is particularly persuasive in a drama such as this and Santell's direction heightens the by-then-firmly-entrenched Boles's image as every woman's dream and Miss Harding's profile as the Glamorous Sufferer Par Excellence. Adapter Jane Murfin retained enough of the flavor of the Louis Bromfield novel to assure reasonably literate dialogue and a faithful depiction of the environment of a small midwest town from 1910 to 1930. The small-town types are also realistically depicted, and the settings and art work are thorough.

Miss Harding, one of the screen's more ladylike heroines of the 1930s, was a handsome woman with blonde hair that she usually wore in a severe but becoming backswept style. Her aristocratic beauty graced many such dramas in the early and mid-Thirties, and most creditably. She was also an excellent actress with a stage-trained voice whose timbre enhanced her pictorial image.

John Boles and Ann Harding

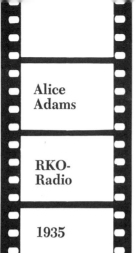

Alice Adams

RKO-Radio

1935

CREDITS: Directed by George Stevens. Produced by Pandro S. Berman. Screenplay by Dorothy Yost and Mortimer Offner. Based on the novel by Booth Tarkington. Adapted for the screen by Jane Murfin. Photographed by Robert De Grasse. Art Direction by Van Nest Polglase. Music by Max Steiner. Edited by Jane Loring.

OPENED at Radio City Music Hall, New York, August 15, 1935. Running time: 99 minutes.

CAST: Katharine Hepburn (Alice Adams); Fred MacMurray (Arthur Russell); Fred Stone (Mr. Adams); Evelyn Venable (Mildred Palmer); Frank Albertson (Walter Adams); Ann Shoemaker (Mrs. Adams); Charles Grapewin (Mr. Lamb); Grady Sutton (Frank Dowling); Hedda Hopper (Mrs. Palmer); Jonathan Hale (Mr. Palmer); Janet McLeod (Henrietta Lamb); Virginia Howell (Mrs. Dowling); Zeffie Tilbury (Mrs. Dresser); Ella McKenzie (Ella Dowling); Hattie McDaniel (Malena).

Katharine Hepburn and Fred MacMurray

Katharine Hepburn and Frank Albertson

Fred MacMurray and Ann Shoemaker

Much has been written about *Alice Adams* as a sociological document and as a realistic study of small-town life, but comparatively little has been made of its strong romantic component. It was conceived by Booth Tarkington in the early 1920s as a serious study of small-town mentality and the frustrated hopes and ambitions of a nice girl with great good will allied with a certain escapist naivete and economic and social deprivation that eventually destroyed her dreams. A film version appeared in 1923; *Alice Adams* in its 1935 RKO incarnation turned out to be quite something else.

For one thing, it gave the talented and distinctive Katharine Hepburn her best opportunity in her then-three-years-in-films and won her an Academy Award nomination (she had received the Oscar in 1933 for a lesser effort, *Morning Glory*). The film also did much for the career of director George Stevens, and sent loanout Fred MacMurray back to his contract studio, Paramount, a bigger name than when he had left.

Max Steiner was again on hand to play on the mood-music heartstrings, and adapter Jane Murfin (Dorothy Yost and Mortimer Offner did the actual screenplay), who was as much of a magician at her typewriter as Steiner was at his orchestral podium, saw to it that the romance was not stinted. The Tarkington novel had ended with Alice Adams, the poor girl who sought social success and love amidst Stickville-Nouveau-Riche snobs, condemned to eke out her life as a clerk-typist after losing the guy of her dreams. Not so the 1935 movie. Everyone concerned decided it just wouldn't do *not* to have Fred MacMurray, 1935's six-foot, curly-haired gift to

Charlie Grapewin and Fred Stone

Katharine Hepburn

*Ann Shoemaker, Fred MacMurray, Frank Albertson,
Katharine Hepburn and Fred Stone*

Fred Stone and Katharine Hepburn

*Hedda Hopper, Jonathan Hale, Fred MacMurray
and Evelyn Venable*

the ladies, tell Miss Hepburn "I love you, Alice," complete with heavy fadeout clinch. Considering the myriad assaults on his character's sensibilities at the

hands of her family, to say nothing of his miraculous forbearance in the face of Alice's at times grotesque pretensions and assorted vagaries, the novel's ending seems the more logical one, with Arthur Russell abandoning hapless Alice and her cloddish family to their respective fates.

But considering the 1935 film audience, made up in large part of frustrated women bored with their husbands and lovelorn girls looking for the Perfect Prince, it would have been the grossest of misdemeanors to have kept wistful Miss Hepburn from the arms of stalwart Mr. MacMurray—the watchword, at least at the fadeout, being: Realism and Tarkington be damned!

All this aside, *Alice Adams* seen today is in many aspects as affecting a film as it was in 1935. There is much poignancy in the Murfin-Yost-Offner screenplay, with Hepburn effectively displayed as a girl of somewhat refined sensibility who is burdened with an improvident and obtuse family. She aspires to the love of Fred MacMurray, who plays with an awareness and sensitivity one doesn't usually ascribe to this actor. Her efforts to counteract her unfortunate family background and win the boy of her dreams are not without dramatic force, and are conveyed by director Stevens with a gentle compassion that at times becomes lyrical.

Hepburn's first meeting with MacMurray at the ball, in which her pathetic efforts to appear chic are ruined by her brother's vulgarities, is put across with an interesting blend of realism and romance, and in the scene in which Hepburn returns from the ball (to which she had been invited only because of the condescension of a rich school friend) to the mean little house, where she goes to her bedroom and then weeps, the audience is on her side all the way. Even the famous dinner-party sequence, with MacMurray attempting valiantly to conceal his dismay at the gaucheries of her bumbling family (to say nothing of Hattie McDaniel's hilarious gaffes as the part-time maid) does not break the romantic mood.

The important point about *Alice Adams* is that it has emotional immediacy. The audience is caught up in it, becomes a part of the doings. Too many films produced in 1974 offer only the arid experience of looking up at a screen watching people and events to which one is essentially noncommitted. Pictures like *Alice Adams* committed the audience. And illogical plotting, occasionally forced situations, grotesque overstatements do not vitiate its total effect. *Alice Adams* is romantic among other reasons because the girl wins the boy despite all human logic and in the film's insistence that sheer determination will carry someone to a better, fuller life—again a questionable assertion. But the total works because many talented people decided that it would. Yes, Hepburn, Stevens, Murfin, Steiner and even Mr. MacMurray, who outdid himself in this, were in there pitching—which demonstrates gratifyingly that there is an exception—in fact many exceptions—to all and any rules.

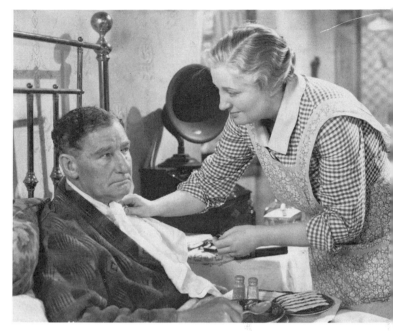

Fred Stone and Ann Shoemaker

Katharine Hepburn and Grady Sutton

These
Three

Samuel
Goldwyn
United
Artists

1936

CREDITS: Directed by William Wyler. Produced by Samuel Goldwyn. Screenplay by Lillian Hellman, based on her play, "The Children's Hour." Photographed by Gregg Toland. Edited by Daniel Mandell. Music by Alfred Newman. Assistant Director, Walter Mayo.

OPENED at the Rivoli Theatre, New York, March 18, 1936. Running time: 93 minutes.

CAST: Miriam Hopkins (Martha Dobie); Merle Oberon (Karen Wright); Joel McCrea (Dr. Joseph Cardin); Catherine Doucet (Mrs. Lily Mortar); Alma Kruger (Mrs. Tilford); Bonita Granville (Mary Tilford); Marcia Mae Jones (Rosalie); Carmencita Johnson (Evelyn); Margaret Hamilton (Agatha); Marie Louise Cooper (Helen Burton); Mary Ann Durkin (Lois); Walter Brennan (Taxi Driver).

Merle Oberon, Joel McCrea and Miriam Hopkins

When the play *The Children's Hour* debuted on Broadway in 1934, it was described as a work that would never reach the screen. A brilliantly written, trenchantly acted study of libelous assertions made by a student at a girls' school against two women teachers, whom she accuses of lesbianism, the play made quite a stir. Lillian Hellman, the author, determined to bring it to the screen, and though the then all-powerful Hays Office and the equally potent Production Code rejected the theme as unacceptable for film audiences, Miss Hellman came up with a different treatment which they approved. She showed it to Samuel Goldwyn, who expressed his liking for it. Shortly he had it scheduled for 1936 release.

What Miss Hellman had done was to concentrate on the lying girl and the damage her mendacities did to others. She eliminated the lesbian overtones and instead had the girl lie about two teachers (Miriam Hopkins and Merle Oberon) and their alleged rivalry for the love of the school doctor (Joel McCrea). The basis of the libel in the new version was the girl's insistence that Miss Hopkins and McCrea had "carried on" in an upstairs bedroom while the students slept nearby.

Hollywood gossip of the prerelease period had it that Goldwyn and Miss Hellman, though credited with the best of intentions, would come a cropper with a screenplay that from all indications would be hopelessly denatured. But the result proved a surprise.

For the biting, bitter, melodramatic stage depiction of malicious gossip and lesbian undercurrents became on the screen a haunting, tender romance, a beautiful study of unrequited love, and a telling rendition of the torments of triangular passion. Greeted by the 1936 reviewers with such encomiums as "stirring," "mature," "powerful," the picture displayed a creative vitality and a delicate sensibility uniquely its own.

In addition to Miss Hellman's well-written screenplay, *These Three* boasted other assets. William Wyler gave his top directorial performance up to that date, probing the characters with the unique combination of sensitivity and incisiveness that became over the years a Wyler trademark. Samuel Goldwyn gave the film all the production gloss and careful mounting for which he was noted, and Gregg Toland photographed it creatively. Alfred Newman provided one of his loveliest scores, admirably suited to the mood of the proceedings, and catching not only the nuances of the ominous evil, but of the romantic yearning that is so much a part of this sensitive film.

Miriam Hopkins's Martha, product of an unhappy childhood with an egoistic actress-aunt, falls in love with Joe (McCrea) but he is unconscious of her feelings, being himself enamored of Miss Oberon's Karen, who returns his love wholeheartedly. One unforgettable scene has Joe, tired after a day of medical rounds, falling asleep on a couch as he talks to Martha in an upstairs bedroom. Martha

Marcia Mae Jones and Miriam Hopkins

William Wyler directing Merle Oberon and Bonita Granville. Samuel Goldwyn in rear

Marcia Mae Jones and Bonita Granville

Bonita Granville and Joel McCrea

Miriam Hopkins, Joel McCrea and Merle Oberon

simply sits in an armchair, her head against its back, looking with longing reflectiveness at Joe as the hours pass—a highly effective scene, and one of many which make *These Three* Miss Hopkins's finest performance.

Miss Oberon was glowing and lovely, and though Bonita Granville, by general agreement did not match the menacing malice of Florence McGee in the stage version, she was most effective as Mary Tilford, the girl whose lies about McCrea and Miss Hopkins set off a chain reaction of destructive scandal that causes the parents to withdraw their girls from the school and reduces the teacher-owners to failure, idleness and encroaching despair.

Granville's lie is sustained by fellow student Marcia Mae Jones, a weak, suggestible child whom Granville blackmails into supporting her story (she knew the other girl had stolen a watch). The three accused go to Mrs. Tilford (Alma Kruger in her finest performance), Granville's grandmother, to force the truth, but fail, since she believes her granddaughter's libel.

Added emotional complications ensue when a tortured, depressed Oberon begins to suspect the nature of McCrea's relationship with Hopkins, though they try to persuade her otherwise. Hopkins, in one of the more moving sequences, confesses her longstanding unrequited love for McCrea to Oberon. Finally Hopkins goes away but not before she has forced a confession from Marcia Mae Jones that exonerates all three and brings a chastened Mrs. Tilford to her knees.

Meanwhile Oberon has sent McCrea away, but when she receives a message from Hopkins, relayed via Mrs. Tilford, she goes to join him in Vienna. The film is replete with many fine scenes: the highly tense confrontation of "These Three" with Mrs. Tilford; the sequences involving the malicious student, the love scenes between McCrea and Oberon, and their final reunion in Vienna.

In 1962 Wyler remade *These Three* under its original title, *The Children's Hour*. Since censorship had meanwhile relaxed, he followed the story line of the play. The change, surprisingly, was not for the better though the treatment was more honest, but Audrey Hepburn, James Garner and Shirley MacLaine, as the teacher who belatedly realizes her lesbian tendencies, were not up to the standard of the earlier leads, and the 1962 story line, lesbianism and all, somehow lacked the power, and certainly the romantic sensibility, of the poignant 1936 version.

Bonita Granville (on couch), Marcia Mae Jones at left. At right, Merle Oberon and Joel McCrea

Joel McCrea, Alma Kruger, Merle Oberon and Miriam Hopkins

45

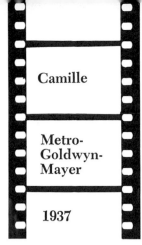

Camille

Metro-Goldwyn-Mayer

1937

CREDITS: Directed by George Cukor. Produced by Irving Thalberg. Screenplay by Zoe Akins, Frances Marion and James Hilton. Adapted from the novel and play. *La Dame Aux Camélias* by Alexandre Dumas. Photographed by William Daniels. Edited by Margaret Booth.

OPENED at the Capitol Theatre, New York, January 22, 1937. Running time: 109 minutes.

CAST: Greta Garbo (Marguerite Gautier); Robert Taylor (Armand Duval); Lionel Barrymore (Monsieur Duval); Elizabeth Allan (Nichette); Jessie Ralph (Nanine); Henry Daniell (Baron de Varville); Lenore Ulric (Olympe); Laura Hope Crews (Prudence); Rex O'Malley (Gaston); Russell Hardie (Gustave); E. E. Clive (Saint Gaudens); Douglas Walton (Henri); Marion Ballou (Corinne); Joan Brodel (Marie Jeanette); June Wilkins (Louise); Fritz Leiber, Jr. (Valentin); Elsie Edmonds (Mademoiselle Duval).

Camille is a perfect illustration of what can be done with cinematic romance when star, director, script, music, direction and production are all working in flawless alliance. And with Greta Garbo as the centerpiece of a picture that sustains her in all departments, failure is unthinkable.

Much has been written of *Camille*, and Garbo's performance in it. Certainly it is the apotheosis of romance. Director George Cukor, who had a special knack for bringing out the best in women stars, here guides the matchless Garbo to her finest performance, and cameraman William Daniels, who photographed her creatively and with an instinctive understanding of her pictorial uniqueness, through most of her two dozen films, makes of this stint of his a work of art.

Nor is Miss Garbo let down by scriptwriters Frances Marion, Zoe Akins and James Hilton, who skillfully adapted the timeworn story. The 1937 screen incarnation of this tragic and ornamental tale of an extravagant, feckless, Parisian butterfly who scales heights of nobility and self-immolation under the bittersweet influences of true love, highlighted the story of the lady of the camellias as never before—and a whole new generation fell in love with her.

Of course Garbo, with her unique ambience and special flavor, was the indispensable element in giving so florid and essentially old-fashioned a tale a validity and a prescience that 1937 audiences would accept. And with Cukor to guide her (she had seldom been so fortunate in directors) and her old standby Daniels to invest her with the imagery and effulgence of an angel come to earth, she gave her devotees a show so potent in its artistry that *Camille* is revived again—and again—and again, and in theatres as often as on TV.

Like other well-wrought films, *Camille* does not date, and like all true works of art it bears continued examination, for one finds something new in it each time.

Under the MGM aegis from 1926 to 1941 Miss Garbo became the screen's most enduring legend, all things to all kinds of audiences, a lady of tantalizing mysteries and fragile illusions. Considered by many to be the screen's all-time best actress, she has been far and away its most discussed, and all kinds of books keep coming out on her, all the more amazing in view of the little factual information

Robert Taylor and Greta Garbo

Greta Garbo and Robert Taylor

Greta Garbo and Robert Taylor

on her and her almost pathologically reclusive lifestyle, which even at age sixty-eight she maintains rigidly.

There has been much discussion of Garbo's sexual magic, her romantic excitement, her gorgeous sensuality and haunting languor, but I have always felt that like all true artists she is essentially a mystic. The core of her delicate art has nothing of the world about it; she seems removed in time, as well as in spirit, from the realities of this or any era; she is in the world but not of it.

But her languor conceals a warm humanity; her smile is like a sunbeam; she seems to combine and contain all the humor and sadness and wry incongruities of the human condition in her best performances. (Much of what she was given to do was unworthy of her artistry.) Hers was not the effective-

Greta Garbo and Lionel Barrymore

Greta Garbo and Elizabeth Allan

ness of studio artifice or of polished technique; her professionalism was always natural and instinctive, her inimitable gestures and inflections guided by the unerring truthfulness that only a gifted instinctual actress can command.

Relying as she did on inspiration rather than technical resource, she could hold her own with proficient, craftsmenlike actors such as Henry Daniell, who plays her protector in *Camille*, and so all-encompassing was her art that the callow and relatively inexperienced actor that Robert Taylor was at twenty-five found himself caught up, by a strange alchemy, in her ambience and gave more than his usual capacities permitted.

Like all true mystics, she has established subtle barriers between herself and others, in great performances like *Camille* as in her private dealings.

Some know the mysticism of self-sacrifice for, and commitment to, their fellow man; Garbo's is the mysticism of the inner life, where dreams shape themselves to the soul's desire. She shared with the world some of her dreams, in masterpieces like *Camille*, and thus made her contribution to humankind.

The story of Camille seems hackneyed via literal recapitulation, but with the mounting it received in that 1937 production, and the combined efforts of the individual talents who benefited it incalculably, it took on a freshness that holds up well through the thirty-seven years since its initial release.

Garbo in *Camille* is the Parisian courtesan who for all her extravagance, coquetries, shallow maneuverings and cynicism, is at heart an idealist and a person of basic integrity. In the Armand of Robert

Rex O'Malley, Lenore Ulric, Laura Hope Crews, Jessie Ralph and Greta Garbo

Henry Daniell and Greta Garbo

Taylor she finds an ideal capable of lifting her up spiritually to her best self; when she abandons the Baron (Daniell), who is keeping her, to go off to the country with him, she does so out of a full heart and consummate sincerity. When Armand's father (Lionel Barrymore) asks her to give him up so as not to jeopardize his future, she grieves mightily but accepts, and when she returns to the Baron, endures Armand's outraged and agonized outbursts, declines finally and fatally into the terminal processes of the tuberculosis which kills her. And in the much-praised death scene, in which she struggles between her joy at seeing Armand again and the sad realization that her death alone will release them both from a relationship as untenable in practical terms as it is enduring in spiritual essence, she offers perhaps the finest expression of her intense cinematic mystique.

And that dialogue! For all its Victorian flow and voluminous phrasing, it rings true in poetic terms: "Armand has taught me that all love is not selfish, nor goodness dull, nor men faithless. . . . Let me love you; let me live for you; don't let's ask more from Heaven than that—God might get angry. . . . I don't suppose you can understand Monsieur, how someone, unprotected as you say I am, can be lifted above selfishness by sentiments so delicate and pure. . . ."

Camille is a poetic masterpiece, Garbo's enduring memorial of her art at its finest.

Jessie Ralph, Greta Garbo and Laura Hope Crews

Russell Hardie, Greta Garbo, Robert Taylor and Elizabeth Allan

Greta Garbo, Rex O'Malley, Jessie Ralph

Robert Taylor and Greta Garbo

51

Lost Horizon

Columbia

1937

CREDITS: Produced and directed by Frank Capra. Screenplay by Robert Riskin, based on the novel by James Hilton. Art direction by Stephen Goosson. Musical score by Dmitri Tiomkin. Musical direction by Max Steiner. Photographed by Joseph Walker. Aerial photography by Elmer Dyer. E. Roy Davidson and Gonafe Corsa, Special Effects, Camera. C. C. Coleman, Assistant Director. Gene Havlick and Gene Milford, Editors. Costumes by Ernst Dryden. Interior decorations by Babs Johnstone. Voices by Hall Johnson Choir.

OPENED at the Globe Theatre, New York, March 3, 1937, on a two-a-day performance basis. Running time: 118 minutes.

CAST: Ronald Colman (Robert Conway); Jane Wyatt (Sandra); Edward Everett Horton (Lovett); John Howard (George Conway); Thomas Mitchell (Barnard); Margo (Maria); Isabel Jewell (Gloria); H. B. Warner (Chang); Sam Jaffe (The High Lama); Hugh Buckler (Lord Gainsford); David Torrence (Prime Minister).

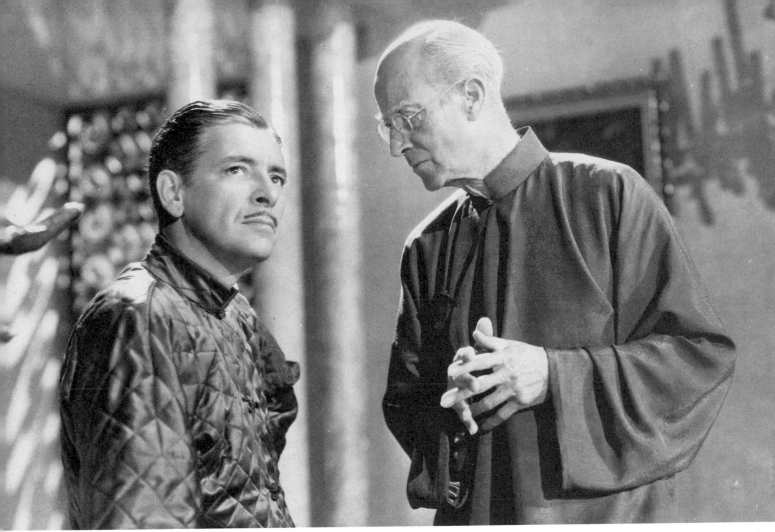

Ronald Colman and H. B. Warner

Lost Horizon is widely considered Frank Capra's—and Ronald Colman's—cinematic highwater mark. There is no denying that this first film transcription of the James Hilton novel is a whale of a movie—inspirational, exciting, well acted, unusual, a film with a "message" all audiences found not only palatable but fantastically entertaining as well.

Everything clicks here: Robert Riskin's screenplay, Dimitri Tiomkin's music, Stephen Goosson's clever art direction, Joseph Walker's photography, a special effects department that went all-out (and it shows) and a story that left 1937 viewers—and those who have viewed it since—in a lasting, warm glow.

The story of a British diplomat who evacuates Europeans from Baskul during an insurrection, finds their plane has been mysteriously redirected, and comes upon the magic land of Shangri-La, lost in the Tibetan wastes, is as well known as any of the great classics. And the message of Shangri-La, imparted by its Grand Lama (Sam Jaffe), has universal appeal. For this holy man, a former Capuchin friar who came to the fabulous retreat from Europe in 1734, and is now over 200 years old, has conceived of Shangri-La as a repository that harbors all that is civilized, good, true and beautiful, against the time when the strong and the evil and the rapacious have devoured each other and the meek come into their

own. He has founded a great library, has gathered art treasures, his people live to a great age, the climate is serene, the environment stately and beautiful.

Too beautiful—and too good to be true, Colman finally decides, at the urging of his impatient younger brother, John Howard, who wants the beautiful Margo, whom he has found at Shangri-La, to leave with them. When they start down the icy mountain she ages to past seventy—it seems that is her true age, and Howard goes mad and jumps to his death. Which gives you some idea of the strangeness and wonder of *Lost Horizon*.

Sam Jaffe as the High Lama who wants Robert Conway (Colman) to succeed him and has had him brought to Shangri-La for just that purpose, portrays an ethereal, mystic, saintly character and in his few scenes he is most effective, as is H. B. Warner as Chang, the "prime minister" of the retreat, who dispenses a strange blend of oriental-style wisdom and shrewd psychology.

Capra directed the film with pace, color, excitement and surprise always in mind; the picture moves at a steady clip, and even the love scenes between Colman and novitiate Jane Wyatt (no, she's not seventy, she's thirty-seven) are blended into the flow so that they slow down the doings not a bit.

'Lost Horizon'' set. Ronald Colman and Jane Wyatt in foreground

H. B. Warner (Center) greets Ronald Colman, John Howard, Edward
Everett Horton and Thomas Mitchell

Ronald Colman

Once he has left Shangri-La, Conway's lot is a bitter and hard one; he is lost in the snows, barely escapes alive when he stumbles into a peasant village. And too late he realizes that he never should have left. Back he goes, once more, to succeed the Lama, who has since died, and find happiness with a waiting Miss Wyatt.

The supporting cast is uniformly excellent: Edward Everett Horton as the fussy paleontologist; Thomas Mitchell as the rogue in flight from the law, Isabel Jewell as the pathetic prostitute whose health has been undermined.

It cost about two million dollars to make *Lost Horizon* late in 1936—one can easily conjecture what such a film would cost today.

A musical version of *Lost Horizon* was produced in 1973, and the less said about it the better. Ross Hunter overproduced the newer version, and Peter Finch and others delegated to match the magic of Colman and company never got within hailing distance. An uneasy blend of not-very-tuneful song and dull romanticizing, the 1973 *Lost Horizon* did not help the legend of the 1937 masterpiece—for which the only conceivable antidote is frequent revival of one of Capra's finest pictures and one of Ronald Colman's finest cinematic hours.

Ronald Colman, Thomas Mitchell, Edward Everett Horton, Isabel Jewell, John Howard (on floor)

Margo and Ronald Colman

Jane Wyatt and Ronald Colman

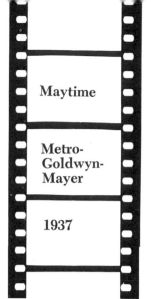

Maytime

Metro-Goldwyn-Mayer

1937

CREDIT: Directed by Robert Z. Leonard. Produced by Hunt Stromberg. Based on the play by Rida Johnson Young. Screenplay by Noel Langley. Music by Sigmund Romberg with added music, musical adaptations and direction by Herbert Stothart. Special lyrics by Bob Wright and Chet Forrest. Photographed by Oliver T. Marsh. Edited by Conrad Nervig. Sound Effects by Douglas Shearer. Gowns by Adrian. Opera sequences, William Van Wymetal. Edwin B. Willis and Fredric Huke, Associate Art Directors. Adaptations of music by Tschaikovsky, Delibes, Wagner, Bellini and others.

OPENED at the Capitol Theatre, New York, March 18, 1937. Running time: 133 minutes.

CAST: Jeanette MacDonald (Marcia Mornay—Miss Morrison); Nelson Eddy (Paul Allison); John Barrymore (Nazaroff); Herman Bing (Archipenco); Tom Brown (Kip); Lynne Carver (Barbara); Rafaela Ottiano (Ellen); Charles Judels (Cabby); Paul Porcasi (Trentini); Sig Rumann (Fanchon); Walter Kingsford (Rudyard); Guy Bates Post (Louis Napoleon); Edgar Norton (Secretary); Anna Demetrio (Madame Fanchon); Iphigenie Castiglioni (Empress Eugenie); Joan Le Sueur (Maypole dancer); Russell Hicks (Voice Coach); Frank Puglia (Orchestra Conductor); Harry Davenport, Harry Hughes, Howard Hickman, Robert C. Fischer (Opera Directors).

Rafaela Ottiano and Jeanette MacDonald

Lynne Carver and Tom Brown

Maytime, the third of the nine films Jeanette MacDonald and Nelson Eddy did together from 1935 to 1942, was their finest effort, and for many reasons.

They had the benefit of Robert Z. Leonard's direction; a strong, believable, human story based on the play by Rida Johnson Young with music by Sigmund Romberg; the added musical inspirations and adaptations of Herbert Stothart, who did for MGM what Max Steiner had done for RKO and Warners; superior photography by Oliver Marsh; a screenplay by Noel Langley that was literate, intelligent and tailored to the stars' personalities; above all the most sumptuous mounting that MGM artisans could provide—and by 1937 that was nothing to sneer at.

Nor did the lovely and talented Miss MacDonald ever appear to more supreme advantage; her makeup, her gowns, the careful photography of the wizard Marsh, the affecting scenes and rousing, bravura musical numbers showcased her as never before or since.

The world of the 1970s is poorer for the loss of Jeanette MacDonald, who died in 1965, and for that matter, the loss of the golden-voiced Nelson Eddy, who followed her in death in 1967, and who never seemed quite himself when paired with other singing stars, so strong was the MacDonald-Eddy chemistry.

In the earlier film period, Miss MacDonald tended toward the baroque and overblown in both her singing and acting, but she gradually refined her stage technique into a mystique fascinatingly and arrestingly cinematic. One has only to look at *Maytime*, the peak of her film incarnation, to gauge the quality of her performances in her great period—it is restrained yet eloquent, feeling, yet leashed and controlled.

John Barrymore was also in *Maytime*, as the impresario Nazaroff, who guides MacDonald's Marcia Mornay to operatic success in Paris and then asks her hand in marriage. Though she accepts him out of gratitude for all he has done, she is not in love, and the emotional void is filled when by accident she encounters singing student Nelson Eddy in a Latin Quarter bistro. They have an idyllic, brief period together and discover their mutual love, but

Nelson Eddy and Jeanette MacDonald

John Barrymore and Charles Judels

Nelson Eddy and Jeanette MacDonald

loyalty to Nazaroff takes precedence over her love and need for Paul Allison (Eddy) and for the next seven years she climbs to the heights of European opera fame as Nazaroff's wife while mourning her lost love.

Seven years later, in America, she finds herself singing opposite Paul, who has made a creditable, if not spectacular, career as an opera singer, and their mutual love is rekindled, to the chagrin of Nazaroff. When Marcia asks her husband for her freedom, he goes to Paul's apartment and kills him in a jealous fury. Paul survives only long enough to die in Marcia's arms.

The story begins with a prologue and ends with an epilogue, both featuring Miss MacDonald as an old lady, living in obscurity as "Miss Morrison," sadly dreaming of her lost love, and counseling a young girl with singing ambitions (Lynne Carver in her first screen role) to forget about career strivings and settle for the young man (Tom Brown) who loves her and whom she loves. This Miss Carver does, and when they go off together, Miss Mac-Donald's heart fails and her youthful shade joins that of Eddy, like the closing scene of *Smilin'*

The Maypole

Through, which however, as presented here, has a freshness and immediacy all its own.

The operatic montages covering Miss MacDonald's peregrinations to various European capitals are skillful and ingenuous, and the adaptations of music by Tchaikovsky, Delibes, Wagner, Bellini and others are skillfully introduced—especially in a fictional opera, called *Czaritsa*, ostensibly written for Miss MacDonald by one Trentini (Paul Porcasi) but actually based on lovely Tchaikovsky melodies. Regardless of its musical origin, this final opera proves exciting to watch, as MacDonald and Eddy sing their hearts out, rising to a crescendo of frustrated musical passion that transfixes the audience and stabs onlooker Barrymore to the heart—one of the most cinematic scenes ever contrived, backed up by all the opulence and pageantry MGM could summon.

Maytime holds up beautifully with the years (the screen version bears scant relation to the original 1917 stage operetta which starred Peggy Wood); it has emotional immediacy, sumptuous mounting, creative freshness, and showcases the lovely Miss MacDonald and the stalwart Mr. Eddy at their zenith.

Nelson Eddy singing in Czaritsa

Stella Dallas

Samuel Goldwyn- United Artists

1937

CREDITS: Directed by King Vidor. Produced by Samuel Goldwyn. Screenplay by Harry Wagstaff Gribble and Gertrude Purcell, based on the novel by Olive Higgins Prouty. Production Associate, Merritt Hulburd. Photographed by Rudolph Mate. Music by Alfred Newman. Edited by Sherman Todd.

OPENED at Radio City Music Hall, New York, August 5, 1937. Running time: 104 minutes.

CAST: Barbara Stanwyck (Stella Dallas); John Boles (Stephen Dallas); Anne Shirley (Laurel Dallas); Barbara O'Neil (Helen Morrison); Alan Hale (Ed Munn); Marjorie Main (Mrs. Martin); Edmund Elton (Mr. Martin); George Walcott (Charlie Martin); Gertrude Short (Carrie Jenkins); Tim Holt (Richard Grosvenor III); Nella Walker (Mrs. Grosvenor); Bruce Satterlee (Con); Jimmy Butler (Con Grown-up); Jack Egger (Lee); Dickie Jones (John); Ann Shoemaker (Miss Phillibronn).

Stella Dallas was one of Olive Higgins Prouty's more successful novels, and when it was published in 1923 it swept the country. By 1924 Mrs. Leslie Carter was starring in a stage version, and its movie advent in 1925 saw Belle Bennett, Ronald Colman and Lois Moran, under Henry King's direction, expertly manipulating the collective heartstrings of the nation.

Surprisingly enough, considering the theme's perennial appeal, there was no talkie remake until 1937. Samuel Goldwyn, who had produced the original film, took it out and dusted it off for another round, this time with King Vidor directing and Barbara Stanwyck, John Boles and Anne Shirley in the Bennett, Colman and Moran roles. Once more Goldwyn had himself a solid hit.

Though manners and mores in America had changed significantly between 1923 and 1937—to say nothing of changes between 1937 and 1974—*Stella Dallas* has never lost its intrinsic appeal—and for all the fact that even in 1937 Stella as a character was somewhat old-hat, the theme of mother love, which has always enjoyed a timeless dramatic urgency, prevailed, the love of mother for child and child for mother being in a spiritual and platonic sense one of the most fundamental and basic romances of humanity. Hence the continuing magic of *Stella Dallas*.

In fact, when seen at theatre revivals and on television in recent years, the 1937 *Stella Dallas* comes across as so superior, in dramatic tension and solid emotional values, to most of the current product, to say nothing of much of the product of its own era, that it invariably seems fresh and new.

There are, of course, basic universals of the human condition in this theme. And in the 1937 picture, Barbara Stanwyck gave the finest performance of her career, bringing Stella to life with a vivid reality and a deeply felt humanity.

Also on hand was John Boles, who seemed to figure more often than not in "woman-oriented" dramas drenched in tears. This time he was not so much a causative factor in the sorrows set forth but rather their passive victim, a departure for him. And Anne Shirley as the gentle-spirited, loyal daughter, offered the best performance of her career.

The story, so familiar after over fifty years, has Stella, the crude harridan with the heart of gold, marrying Stephen Dallas (Boles), a man of refined sensibility and good background, while he has tem-

porarily exiled himself to a small Massachusetts industrial town. It seems his father, a prominent socialite, had committed suicide leaving his son and heir penniless. This had aborted Boles's plan to marry fellow patrician Barbara O'Neil, who wound up with someone else. Stella is temporarily bedazzled by Stephen's "class," having read in the Sunday supplements of the society tragedy, but soon the disparities in their upbringing and educational-cultural level become apparent, and Stella refuses to go to New York with Stephen when he gets a better job, preferring to stay in the little town where she can consort with her rough-mannered, lowbrow friends. But she is a loving, exemplary mother to her daughter Laurel, watches over her tenderly, makes all her clothes, gives her every attention.

Stella is courted by crude but good-hearted Ed Munn (Alan Hale) but informs him there is no room for anyone else in her life but her daughter. Stephen pays occasional visits and is shocked by the behavior of her rowdy friends, fearing for his daughter's welfare. When Laurel's teachers note Ed Munn's offensive conduct on a train while in Stella's company, they jump to the wrong conclusions and their children snub Laurel's birthday party.

Laurel pays a visit to her father in New York and being a refined, intelligent girl, she is impressed

Barbara Stanwyck and Anne Shirley

Barbara Stanwyck

with the now-widowed Barbara O'Neil, with whom Boles has resumed, and her handsome sons. Boles wants to divorce Stanwyck to marry O'Neil, but Stanwyck refuses. She takes their daughter to a fashionable resort on Boles's money, and there, coincidentally, learns that her crude plebeian manners and flamboyant overdressing are hampering her daughter's chances for a better life and marriage to the aristocratic boy (Tim Holt) she loves.

She then shows her true mettle by rising to the occasion. She visits O'Neil and in one of the picture's more affecting scenes, she asks her to take her daughter into her home in exchange for the divorce she is now willing to grant so that Boles and O'Neil can marry. When Shirley objects to the arrangement she stages a vulgar scene to alienate the girl and pretends she now wants her own life, ostensibly with Hale, by then a drunken bum. When she writes her daughter that she has gone off to South America with him, Shirley returns tearfully to Boles and O'Neil, who of course sees through the mother's stratagem.

Comes the daughter's wedding to the young man of her heart, and O'Neil sees to it that it is staged by a drawing-room window of the townhouse so that people outside can look in. And there is Stanwyck,

drenched in the rain, peering in lovingly at the ceremony while a policeman urges the onlookers to move on. And when the groom has given the new bride his kiss, she turns and marches down the street with a look of exalted triumph on her face.

An irresistible story, and Stanwyck, who for several years prior to this break had been victimized by a series of inferior pictures, won an Academy Award nomination, losing unaccountably to Luise Rainer's *The Good Earth*.

Stella Dallas has many moving scenes that contain as much emotional validity in 1974 as they did in 1937. Touching indeed are she and Barbara O'Neil as they sit together in the latter's elegant drawing room and O'Neil slowly comes to realize the total unselfishness of this crude, unschooled woman. Her aristocratic coldness and reserve melt gradually into the elemental concern of one mother for another, one woman for another, and when Stanwyck tells O'Neil how wonderful her daughter is, O'Neil gently replies, "I know she is—and I know she didn't get it all from her father." Stanwyck lying in a sleeping berth on a train listening to cruelly thoughtless young girls laughing about her grotesque appearance and behavior at the fashionable resort. Laurel in the berth above fears her mother has heard, and

Barbara Stanwyck

*Anne Shirley and
Barbara Stanwyck*

comes down to sleep with her. Stanwyck, pretending that she has been asleep, holds her girl in her arms, her eyes wide open, stricken, staring, groping toward the ultimate sacrifice, seeing as she now does that she has become more of a liability than an asset to the daughter she loves more than anything else in life. And when Shirley tells Stanwyck during one of Boles's infrequent visits that he is waiting in the living room to take their daughter to New York for Christmas, Stanwyck goes into the bedroom and mindful that Boles hates ostentatious clothing, cuts off the frills and furbelows from one of her less garish dresses, tones down her makeup, and goes out to meet him to make one last stand for happiness, for she now wants him back.

But Hale ruins it by appearing in a drunken condition, and Boles, who had been melting toward the chastened Stanwyck and had planned to include her in their celebration, coldly withdraws again into his shell, departs with their daughter, and leaves her standing dejectedly in the hall. Stanwyck at the birthday party to which no one comes; she and her stricken, bewildered daughter take plates from the table, rearranging as each regret comes by messenger, and finally sit down alone together to eat the ice cream and cake—one of the movies' most famous sequences. And Stanwyck's myriad expressions as she watches her daughter's wedding in the rain; she puts thumb to mouth with almost childlike delight at what she is witnessing; slowly she inclines her head to one side, carried away by this fulfillment of all her dreams for her daughter; her eyes glow with happy tears—and then that triumphant stride down the street—and the last things you see in the film are the Stanwyck eyes, glowing, radiant, the perfect expression of self-sacrificing motherhood fulfilled.

Alfred Newman contributed a rich score to the film, and it fittingly enhances the richness of mood in scene after scene. The Goldwyn taste is everywhere present, the script is literate and polished, and King Vidor's direction is sensitive, seasoned and sure.

Stella Dallas works, in this or any era, because it plumbs the deep wells of the human heart, propounds timeless truths, consummately legitimizes human concepts that in less sure hands would seem soggy and maudlin but are here valid and inevitable.

Barbara O'Neil and Barbara Stanwyck

63

CREDITS: Directed by W. S. Van Dyke II. Produced by Hunt Stromberg. Screenplay by Claudine West, Donald Ogden Stewart and Ernest Vajda. Based in part on the book by Stefan Zweig. Music by Herbert Stothart. Song, "Amour, Eternal Amour," by Herbert Stothart, Chet Forrest and Bob Wright. Art Direction by Cedric Gibbons. Montage by Slavko Vorkapich. Dances by Albertina Rasch. Photographed by William Daniels. Edited by Robert J. Kern.

OPENED at the Astor Theatre, New York, August 16, 1938 on a two-a-day performance basis. Running time, 160 minutes.

CAST: Norma Shearer (Marie Antoinette); Tyrone Power (Count Axel Fersen); John Barrymore (Louis XV); Robert Morley (Louis XVI); Anita Louise (Princesse de Lamballe); Joseph Schildkraut (Duc d'Orleans); Henry Stephenson (Count Mercy); Cora Witherspoon (Countess de Noailles); Barnett Parker (Prince de Rohan); Gladys George (Madame du Barry); Reginald Gardiner (Count d'Artois); Albert Dekker (Count de Provence); Alma Kruger (Empress Maria Theresa); Henry Daniell (La Matie); Leonard Penn (Toulon); Joseph Calleia (Drouet); George Meeker (Robespierre); Scotty Beckett (The Dauphin, later "Louis XVII"); Marilyn Knowlden (Princess Therese); Henry Kolker (Court Aide); Horace MacMahon (Rabblerouser); Robert Barrat (Sauce); George Zucco (Governor of the Conciergerie); and Ian Wolfe, John Burton, Mae Busch, Cecil Cunningham, Ruth Hussey, Walter Walker, Claude King, Herbert Rawlinson, Wade Crosby, George Houston, Moroni Olsen, Barry Fitzgerald, Harry Davenport, Olaf Hytten, Anthony Warde, Rafaela Ottiano.

Tyrone Power and Norma She

Norma Shearer and Tyrone Power

Norma Shearer was one of the screen's most talented, glamorous and attractive stars, and though she worked in films for only twenty-two years (1920 to 1942) she left a lasting impact on the Hollywood in which she reigned during the 1930s as a top-drawer glamour symbol. She was also an excellent actress, won one of the first Oscars (for *The Divorcee*) and a number of nominations, one of which

(1938) was for *Marie Antoinette*. Bette Davis beat her out that year with *Jezebel*.

Marie Antoinette had a rather strange history. Miss Shearer's husband, producer Irving Thalberg, who never lived to see it become a screen reality, had purchased the Stefan Zweig book on which it was based some five years before, as a vehicle for his wife. William Randolph Hearst wanted it for Marion Davies; he didn't get it; he also didn't get *The Barretts of Wimpole Street* for Miss Davies. Miss Shearer made that into a 1934 movie and Hearst and Davies packed up their bungalow and

Robert Morley and Norma Shearer

Norma Shearer and Joseph Schildkraut

moved to Warners. A fortune was spent on the film before a foot of it got into the can; a man was sent to France to buy expensive furniture and antiques; no cost was to be spared to make this one of MGM's most opulent films. Script trouble developed, and many hands got into it, but the Claudine West-Donald Ogden Stewart-Ernest Vajda screenplay that finally made the grade had to wait until early January 1938. Mayer was nervous about the cost, and dreaded a protracted schedule which would run it up even more. Sidney Franklin had been Thalberg's choice to direct, but he was thought too slow and painstaking, so the notorious "fast-shooter" W. S. Van Dyke was drafted, and he rushed Shearer and entourage through the picture in ten weeks—quite a feat for a 160-minute film. Shearer would have preferred Franklin but found Van Dyke, from all reports, satisfactory to work with, and the result was a picture that for some strange reason got itself quite disliked in certain critical quarters.

Why, I will never know, for I consider it a masterpiece, and have sat through it twenty-five times over the years. It has dynamism, tremendous sweep; it *moves*, and Van Dyke's shrewd hand is everywhere apparent. (I have always considered Van Dyke an underrated director whose career deserves respectful reevaluation.)

The West-Stewart-Vajda scenes are moving and literate. True, they take a number of liberties with history, but the basics of Marie Antoinette's life and career are there, and the function of a truly good movie is to *entertain*—and that it does.

Some scenes approach cinematic greatness: the grotesque honeymoon night of Shearer and gargantuan Robert Morley (brilliant in his role), a forlorn, impotent dauphin ashamed of his image and of his inability to please the dynasts around him; Shearer's reaction to Madame DuBarry's insult (she sends her a cradle on her second wedding anniversary and bids her fill it). "I will be the brightest highest star in all this court," she tells her fumbling, timid husband who keeps repeating "The king is the king!"

Soon she is surrounded by court fops and dilettantes led by the decadent, scheming Duc d'Orleans (Joseph Schildkraut), meets Fersen (Tyrone Power) at a gaming house, dallies with him, loses a valuable necklace on a wager, and the Austrian ambassador tells her she is the first dauphine to be spoken of as "a wanton."

She humiliates DuBarry at a ball and the king wants to send her back to Austria but dies before fulfilling his threat, and she is Queen. Fersen tells her she used frivolity and sham as shields against loneliness and unhappiness, and that now she must be a worthy queen. As for himself, he is going to America but will love her always. Morley recovers his potency and soon she is brought to bed with two children. But Morley's Louis XVI is a bumbling incompetent, however well-meaning, and cynical old Louis XV – John Barrymore's prediction–"After me the deluge"—is fulfilled.

Van Dyke then pushes the picture briskly

Joseph Schildkraut, Tyrone Power, Anita Louise,
Norma Shearer and Reginald Gardiner

through the horrors of the revolution, the sack of the palace, the abortive attempt to escape to the border, the temple, and eventual execution, first of Morley, then of Shearer.

The power and poignancy of the latter scenes cannot be described adequately: Morley's last night with his family (his rare acting gifts are on brilliant display here, as indeed throughout the film); Shearer's horror and shock at his execution; the loss of her son to the revolutionists; the final terrible wait for death. And when it comes, as she stands slightly dazed as the guillotine knife rises and rises, she sees in beautifully montaged flashback her face as a girl in Austria (the film's first scene) declaring delightedly to her mother, Empress Maria Theresa, "Just think, Mama, I shall be a queen; I shall be Queen of France!"

Miss Shearer dominates the film throughout, not only because scriptwriters, director, and all concerned have focused on her but because her beauty and talent magnetize the attention. It takes a true star to shine amidst so much glittering splendor and mammoth production opulence; there is pageantry; there are revolutionary onslaughts, palace-stormings, court balls, crowded theatre scenes—in all of them the star is the centerpiece.

Special commendation should be given Cedric Gibbons's art direction. The magnificent ballrooms, grand staircases, halls, etc. look as authentic as anything can get outside Versailles itself. Herbert Stothart's music is affecting and tender in the intimate scenes where such is required; rousing, martial, alarumed, triumphantly vital when needed—a tour de force of movie musical expression.

Miss Shearer is well supported: by Joseph Schildkraut's unctuous, sly, poisonously diverse Orleans, one of his finest screen creations; Morley is, as before noted, simply magnificent, and toward the end achieves a humanity and a sympathy in his characterization that puts the audience on his side. Gladys George is an overblown, vulgar Madame DuBarry, but arresting in her few scenes, and John Barrymore is properly cynical, spiritually depleted and crassly unpredictable as Louis XV.

William Daniels's photography and the dances staged by Albertina Rasch are also a delight. *Marie Antoinette* is one of those films one ponders long afterward, savoring certain scenes in memory, recalling an inflection here, a gesture there, a line of dialogue that is particularly sharp and apropos. Well written, well acted, lavishly produced with the full resources of 1938 MGM—and that was full indeed—*Marie Antoinette* is one of the more underrated films of that or any era. But thanks to frequent revivals—and unfortunately frequent TV appearances where it is cruelly cut—the film has gathered a cult coterie, and there is little likelihood that it will lose it. There is one truism more true and pertinent than the oft-repeated "True Art Never Dates" and that is that "True Art Sometimes Gets Belatedly Discovered." So with this Shearer gem.

Norma Shearer

Wuthering Heights

Samuel Goldwyn-United Artists

1939

CREDITS: Directed by William Wyler. Produced by Samuel Goldwyn. Screenplay and adaptation by Ben Hecht and Charles MacArthur. Based on the novel by Emily Brontë. Photographed by Gregg Toland. Music by Alfred Newman. Edited by Daniel Mandell.

OPENED at the Rivoli Theatre, New York, April 13, 1939. Running time: 103 minutes.

CAST: Merle Oberon (Cathy); Laurence Olivier (Heathcliff); David Niven (Edgar Linton); Geraldine Fitzgerald (Isabella); Flora Robson (Ellen Dean); Donald Crisp (Dr. Kenneth); Hugh Williams (Hindley); Leo G. Carroll (Joseph); Cecil Humphreys (Judge Linton); Miles Mander (Lockwood); Romaine Callender (Robert); Cecil Kellaway (Earnshaw); Rex Downing (Heathcliff as a child); Sarita Wooton (Cathy as a child); Douglas Scott (Hindley as a child); Miss Alice Ehlers (Harpsichordist).

David Niven, Merle Oberon, Geraldine Fitzgerald, Flora Robson

Wuthering Heights is among the great classics of the screen today, and is as fresh and moving when seen on television or in a movie-house revival as it was in its release year, 1939. Indeed it burst upon the screen that year as a revelation of what cinema artistry could accomplish in the transcription of a fine novel that had hitherto been regarded as non-cinematic.

Emily Brontë had written a wildly passionate, deeply felt work, published in 1847. It was set against a somber background, the Yorkshire moors, and it was a surprisingly nonsentimental, force-fully wrought tale of a gypsy boy picked up on the streets of Liverpool by Mr. Earnshaw of Wuthering Heights, who brings him to his estate on the edge of the moors. There he grows to manhood, and after his benefactor's death is hated by the son of the house, Hindley, now the master, and loved by Hindley's sister Cathy. Heathcliff, as the boy is called, is a wild, untamable creature, an alien to his environment, primitive, instinctual, hellish in his rages and elemental in his emotions. Cathy's strong attraction to him is counterbalanced by her desire for security and a safe, elegant life, which the neighboring Edgar Linton can provide.

When Heathcliff overhears Cathy tell the housekeeper, Ellen Dean, that it would degrade her to marry him, he disappears, and Cathy, desperately unhappy after his departure, marries Edgar Linton and goes to live at the Grange. But years later Heathcliff returns and a triangular situation develops, with Cathy determined to resist his persistent overtures, though she still loves him. He is now rich and substantial, and has acquired a polished veneer, though his wild black eyes still contain the old Heathcliff, as she realizes. Edgar Linton's sister Isabella falls in love with Heathcliff, who has paid Cathy's dissolute brother Hindley's debts and now rules at Wuthering Heights, which he has purchased. To take revenge on Cathy, Heathcliff marries Isabella, and a fourth partner has been added to the roundelay of emotional torment, with Isabella withering under Heathcliff's postmarital indifference and Cathy dying of a broken heart.

In the film, Heathcliff goes to Cathy as she is dying, and carries her to the window to look out at the crag that in childhood was their "castle." She tells him she will wait for him and that one day they will be reunited. Then she dies.

Distraught, Heathcliff spends the next twenty

Laurence Olivier and Merle Oberon

years mourning Cathy and longing for death. He continues to inflict bitterness and impatient scorn on all he knows and meets until he finally is called by the ghost of Cathy to the moors in the snowy dead of winter and joins her in death at their favorite spot.

Miss Brontë's novel and the movie part company at about the point of Cathy's death, with the Brontë story of the subsequent life and career of the second generation covered at length. Ben Hecht and Charles MacArthur, the scenarists, did a masterly job of capturing the emotional and spiritual essence of the novel, and indeed do a more polished and romantic job than Miss Brontë herself did, *her* aim being to tell a fierce, wild story of a demon walking like a man who fired the emotions of everyone he encountered, and *their* aim being to create in Heathcliff a romantic hero who would draw audiences into movie theatres.

But Miss Brontë's Heathcliff and the Hecht-MacArthur Heathcliff are still spiritually identical; similar emotions and bewitchments taunt both; one of literature's most renowned male characters, the complex, bedeviled, revenge-ridden, love-frustrated

David Niven and Merle Oberon

Heathcliff, is, if anything, enlarged and clarified by his cinematic incarnation. And in the portrayal of Laurence Olivier, he seems a larger than life, highly elemental, perversely charismatic being.

Under the guidance of the talented director William Wyler, Olivier, who had been anything but an international name up to then, and who had languished on the British stage and in mediocre movies for some ten years, found himself a star of world renown upon the picture's release. As the inferior 1971 British remake illustrates, he *is* Heathcliff in the public mind, and will always remain so. Wyler worked diligently with Olivier, toning down his somewhat precious stage mannerisms and deepening and sharpening his characterization. They disagreed at times, and Olivier also had his run-ins with his costar Merle Oberon, but the result, produced under the tasteful aegis of Samuel Goldwyn, delighted all participants, to say nothing of the public, who flocked to see it in droves.

Miss Oberon gave perhaps the best performance of her career as Cathy, the girl who knew she was not made for Edgar Linton's heaven, being in love with a creature, Heathcliff, who seemed straight out of hell. She delineated the tortured confusions of a girl who admires one man, the one she marries, but loves the other, whom she associates with the worst in herself. "I *am* Heathcliff," she tells housekeeper Ellen Dean (Flora Robson) as the thunder

Merle Oberon and Laurence Olivier

rolls and the lighting flashes—and in the end, at the point of death, she offers up her spirit to him, as he offers his to her, living only to follow her in death.

Olivier and Miss Oberon joined the long list of actors who seemed to outdo themselves under Wyler's guiding hand—he had a special knack for getting the best out of artists; for Olivier it meant a whole new career; with this one picture he became an instantly recognizable cult figure and a satisfying windup indeed for the young actor Greta Garbo had rejected six years before for *Queen Christina* because she felt his love scenes lacked dynamism (John Gilbert got the role).

Though shot in California, (though largely with English actors,) the film achieved an amazing verisimilitude to England's Yorkshire, thanks to shrewd location choices. The British themselves paid tribute to its surprisingly authentic ambience. Oddly enough, when they made it in 1971, following the original novel more closely, it didn't compare with the 1939 version, among other reasons being that Timothy Dalton was no Olivier; Anna Calder-Marshall was no Oberon—and Robert Fuest was certainly no Wyler, lacking the Master's discipline, precision, and capacity for taking creative pains.

Among the supporting cast Flora Robson, Miles Mander and Geraldine Fitzgerald, as the hapless Isabella, are particularly outstanding, and David

Niven acquits himself well as Edgar Linton, the well-meaning, kindly but essentially vapid country gentleman who finds himself no match for Heathcliff in the tournaments of love.

An essentially respectful, painstaking, selective retelling of a world-famous classic, the 1939 *Wuthering Heights* offers moviegoers to this day a large serving of elemental, fierce, kinetic romance—romance born in the tortured-yet-dynamic mind and spirit of a reclusive English genius, and told in clarified, illuminating modern terms by a director, Wyler, who is a genius in his own, special mold.

David Niven, Merle Oberon and Geraldine Fitzgerald

The
Old
Maid

Warner
Bros.

1939

CREDITS: Directed by Edmund Goulding. Produced by Hal B. Willis. Associate Producer, Henry Blanke. Screen play by Casey Robinson. Based on the play by Zoe Akins adapted from the novel by Edith Wharton. Photographed by Tony Gaudio. Art Direction by Robert Haas. Music by Max Steiner. Musical direction by Leo F. Forbstein. Orchestral arrangements by Hugo Friedhofer. Costumes by Orry-Kelly. Edited by George Amy.

OPENED at the Strand Theatre, New York, August 11, 1939. Running time: 95 minutes.

CAST: Bette Davis (Charlotte Lovell); Miriam Hopkins (Delia Lovell Ralston); George Brent (Clement Spender); Jane Bryan (Tina); Donald Crisp (Dr. Lanskell); Jerome Cowan (Joe Ralston); James Stephenson (Jim Ralston); Louise Fazenda (Dora); William Lundigan (Lanning Halsey); Cecilia Loftus (Grandmother Lovell); Rand Brooks (Jim Ralston, Jr.); Janet Shaw (Dee Ralston); William DeWolf Hopper (John); Marlene Burnett (Tina as a child); Rod Cameron (Man); Doris Lloyd (Nursemaid); Frederick Burton (Mr. Halsey).

The Old Maid is not only this writer's favorite Bette Davis picture but also his all-time favorite movie. Made in 1939, at the height of Hollywood's (and Miss Davis's) golden era, it is a superb romantic drama with a demoniacal, bittersweet, love-hate quality and a sweeping dramatic élan that few pictures before or since can match. Yet one hears more about Miss Davis's *Dark Victory*, made the same year, or her *Jezebel* (1938) or *Now, Voyager* (1942) or *All About Eve* or *Of Human Bondage* or—well, you name *your* favorite Bette Davis picture.

That flood-tide year, 1939, gave this neglected masterpiece some tough competition, granted. For it was the year of *Wuthering Heights* and *Gone With the Wind* and *Stagecoach* and *Mr. Smith Goes to Washington* and *Goodbye, Mr. Chips* and other blockbusters. Still, it is difficult to understand why, even among the film buffs, *The Old Maid* has not been accorded its just recognition as a cinema classic of the first order, and Bette Davis's finest picture, which I sincerely believe it to be. As far back as 1955, in my Bette Davis career article in the December issue of *Films in Review*, I was hailing this film as representative, to an eminent degree, of the full-bloom quintessence of the Davis mystique. For in it she ran the total range from girlish ingenuousness to an embittered maturity, as a woman unable to acknowledge her child by a lover long dead.

I had taken note throughout the 1930s of Davis's vivid presence. I had admired her in man-eater roles such as *Of Human Bondage* and *Dangerous*. I thought her compelling in *Jezebel* and moving in the gimmicky but poignant *Dark Victory*, but Davis in *The Old Maid* came upon me as a revelation when I first saw it as a boy of sixteen. Here in one comprehensive, superbly professional package, was everything an archetypal Bette Davis movie should be. All the things she had done in the 1931-1939 period had, I then realized, led her to this summit, and after *The Old Maid* I thought her the screen's all-time greatest actress. Despite the sad decline in her roles in recent years, I still do.

The film was excellent, of course, in all departments, benefiting as it did from Edmund Goulding's sensitive direction, an eloquent screenplay from the gifted Casey Robinson, based on the Pulitzer Prize-winning Zoe Akins play from the Edith Wharton

Bette Davis

George Brent and Bette Davis

novel; handsome period art work (1861-1881) by
Robert Haas, and one of Max Steiner's loveliest and
most haunting scores. In short, a sumptuously produced, dramatically compelling, superbly acted tour
de force, a perfect example of the full flowering of
Hollywood's Golden Age, with Miss Davis at what
can only be described as her most majestic.

Until *The Old Maid*, Davis the Bitch was the
chief image she had projected from America's
screens. This film showcased another Davis—the actress of sweeping range threading with infinite art
and instinctual creativity the odd vagaries of love
and hate, bitterness and idealism, aspiration and
frustration. Miriam Hopkins, always a fine actress,
complemented the Davis characterization ably, but
with due credit for her expert playing, it is essentially Miss Davis's picture. She has the showier role
with the wider spectrum of emotions.

The tragic story deals with Charlotte Lovell
(Davis) who in 1861 loved hopelessly and unrequitedly the dashing, magnetic Clem Spender (George
Brent) who regards her with offhand condescension
as "Little Cousin Charlotte" and instead loves Charlotte's cousin Delia (Miriam Hopkins) who is a
self-protective, conventional, security-loving girl and
deserts the charming but irresponsible Clem for a
safe marriage with solid-citizen Philadelphian Jim
Ralston (James Stephenson). Charlotte, who sees

Bette Davis, George Brent and Miriam Hopkins

Jerome Cowan and Bette Davis (a scene that was edited out of final print)

her one and only chance to win, if only by default, the man she has long and hopelessly loved, comforts the heartbroken Clem on the day of Delia's wedding. He turns to her temporarily on the rebound, but without loving her. He then goes off to the Civil War, leaving her with child. The end of the war (1866) finds Charlotte running a home for orphans in which she conceals her daughter by Clem, who had been killed at Vicksburg without marrying her.

Obsessed with her tragic secret, Charlotte has withdrawn into herself. Delia, who still loves the dead Clem but knows nothing of his affair with Charlotte, arranges for Charlotte to marry her brother-in-law Joe Ralston (Jerome Cowan) and Charlotte, seeking to assuage her loneliness, agrees, but on her wedding day, when she confesses the child's existence to Delia in a frantic last-minute attempt to gain advice and consolation, she enrages her cousin. Rendered insupportably jealous by the revelation of Clem's involvement with Charlotte, Delia lies to the bridegroom-to-be. Claiming that Charlotte has lung fever, she succeeds in preventing the marriage.

Charlotte gradually grows into an embittered old maid. She and Clem's child, Tina (Jane Bryan), come to live with Delia after the latter is widowed, and in the subsequent bitter competition for the love of Tina, child of the man both women loved, Delia wins out over Charlotte, whose corroding, guilt-bedeviled secret forces her to foreswear overt affection for her daughter out of fear that the girl may realize that the old maid, "Aunt Charlotte," is actually her mother. Years pass and Tina, purported to be a Civil War orphan of unknown parentage, is nineteen and ready for marriage, but is rejected by the snobbish parents of Lanning Halsey (William Lundigan), the young socialite she loves. Tina has come to hate the dour and forbidding "Aunt Charlotte," who in her mind stands for everything grim, restrictive and love-denying, and instead gives all her love to the motherly and suave but subconsciously revenge-ridden Delia. Delia later adopts Tina, giving her the Ralston name and part of the Ralston fortune, so that she will have the proper background to marry Lanning.

On the night before the wedding, the two women quarrel over the girl. Charlotte almost tells her daughter the truth about her parentage, but in the end sends Delia to her bedroom. "You are the mother she wants and needs tonight," she says forlornly. "She is not mine—just as her father was never really mine," adding wistfully, "At least she was mine—when she was little." In the final scene, on the day of the wedding, Delia asks Tina to give her last kiss to the old maid before she goes off with her young husband.

The plot, while forceful enough in the telling, does not begin to convey the amalgam of creativity, in acting, direction, scoring, photography, screenwriting, the first-rate dramatic tension, romantic power, spiritual catharsis and contrapuntal nuance

Bette Davis

Bette Davis and Miriam Hopkins

Marlene Burnett, Miriam Hopkins and Bette Davis

that this fine picture offers. It has, to a preeminent degree, what I call "confrontation-tension"—two strong spirits at odds to the death—in this instance, spiritual death. The profound, ineffable tenderness, the love-hate contrapuntal synthesis, the unspeakable diabolism of love turned in upon itself, the sense of "the buried life," the masterful juxtaposition of positive and negative, have never been displayed to such effect on the screen. And Robinson's dialogue, complemented by Steiner's deeply affecting score, is poetic. Sample: Davis to Hopkins as they face each other on the staircase the eve of the girl's marriage: "You've thought of him (Clem) when you've thought of her. A woman never stops thinking of the man she loves; she thinks of him in all sorts of unconscious ways—a sunset, an old song, a cameo and chain." Davis in her wedding gown, sitting sadly in an upstairs bedroom while the guests assemble for the ceremony downstairs—she is torn between hope for the imminent marriage that will give her a new lease on life and love, and concern for the nameless child who embodies in her person the true love she has lost forever; her face registers conflicting emotions—and she looks at that point as beautiful as Garbo herself. Davis

a shriveled old spinster, late in the picture, cowering behind a drawing-room door, shawl drawn up close against the cold without and within as she listens to Tina and her young man whispering words of love and communing fervently as only the young can. She stands still and tense, frozen in her aging aloneness, and when she senses the dangerous abandon of Tina's love for Lanning her eyes widen in horror at the prospect of fate repeating itself and she turns and crosses the hall to confront them; Davis withering literally as the girl, enraged at her interference with the love affair, castigates her as a spiteful, dried-up old maid who knows nothing of love. Davis looking down wistfully from an upper hall at the young couples happily dancing; she turns and goes into the bedroom and gently she dances alone, to the strains of a sad and nostalgic waltz. Suddenly she stops, aware in a flash that she is old and withered and alone in a terrible, final, Death-awaiting sense, and she sinks slowly to the sofa by the fire, brokenly whispering the name of the young man long taken from her by death.

An electric, demoniacal scene in mid-film: Davis, six months after the broken marriage, comes to condole with Hopkins, whose husband is dying.

While waiting in the drawing-room, she learns by accident from her almost-husband (by then married to someone else) that Hopkins, in preventing the marriage, had lied to him, ascribing Davis's last-minute unavailability to a recurrence of her supposed "lung-fever" rather than the child's existence. Wild with fury and frustration, Davis rushes into the great hall of the mansion; there she faces a Hopkins grieving for her dying spouse; Davis spits out all her hurt and hatred; then the family doctor comes to tell Hopkins that her husband has just died; all the family and retainers file funeral-style up the great flight of stairs while the camera zeroes in on Davis, who has turned away from the mourners with a look of diabolical rage and frustration on her face counterpointed against the melancholy scene behind her.

And in what emotionally sterile 1974 film do you find a scene like the tender miniature in which Davis, after Hopkins's wedding early in the picture, is comforting the bride's rejected suitor whom she has loved from childhood, and shocks the young man into an awareness of her true feelings for him with the words: "Don't you know that your happiness means more to me than anything else in the world?" When she asks the now-alerted and compassionate object of her love not to laugh at her, he gently replies: "How could I laugh at anyone so sweet, so sincere. . . ."

Bette Davis

The Old Maid was in every sense a film ahead of its time. It offered emotions in depth, the delineations of the buried, interior life that flourishes beneath many an inarticulate exterior, a graphic depiction of Love as the Destroyer as well as the Nurturer of the Human Spirit.

It is a picture for all those who are in love with love, who have derived joy and fulfillment from it as did Tina and her young man, and loneliness and bitterness and eternal aridity from it, as did the old maid who missed its ultimacies. But essentially the mystique of this picture cannot be imparted in mere words; one can recite (as I have) scenes and dialogue and try to convey its consummate artistry, its depth of feeling, the taste and restraint of its execution, the finality of its catharsis, but it has to be experienced. It is one of those pictures that can profitably be seen many times. Like all products of genuine depth and sincere esthetic commitment, it rewards each viewing with something new.

Bette Davis, George Brent and Miriam Hopkins

CREDITS: Directed by Gregory Ratoff. Produced by David O. Selznick for United Artists release. Associate Producer, Leslie Howard. Screenplay by George O'Neil. Based on the screenplay for the 1936 Swedish version by Gosta Stevens and Gustaf Molander. Musical direction by Leo Forbes. Photographed by Gregg Toland. Edited by Hal C. Kern and Francis D. Lyon.

OPENED at Radio City Music Hall, New York, October 5, 1939. Running time: 70 minutes.

CAST: Leslie Howard (Holger Brandt); Ingrid Bergman (Anita Hoffman); Edna Best (Margit Brandt); John Halliday (Thomas Stenborg); Cecil Kellaway (Charles); Enid Bennett (Greta); Ann Todd (Ann Marie); Douglas Scott (Eric); Eleanor Wesselhoeft (Emma); Maria Flynn (Marianne).

Leslie Howard and Ingrid Bergman

Leslie Howard and Edna Best

Intermezzo is best remembered today for its introduction to American audiences of the charming Swedish star Ingrid Bergman, whose luminous personality, as showcased in this film, turned her overnight into a Hollywood star. Produced with taste by David O. Selznick and associate producer Leslie Howard, who also starred, it boasted an affecting screenplay by George O'Neil, who modeled his conception on the original Swedish scenario by Gosta Stevens and Gustaf Molander. Fine camerawork by the talented Gregg Toland and the lush musical scoring directed by Lou Forbes, complemented the stars' work.

The Stevens-Molander Swedish version had been reviewed in New York in late 1937 after a 1936 release in Sweden. It too starred Ingrid Berg-

man, opposite the Swedish star Gosta Ekman, who played the role Leslie Howard took over for the 1939 version. In both, Miss Bergman revealed herself a consummate artist of surpassing physical loveliness, though she was better photographed in the Hollywood version and was helped by technical polish and more tasteful mounting. She was also well directed by Gregory Ratoff, and her chemistry meshed well with Howard's.

Romantic it was, this *Intermezzo* (the 1939 version was titled *Intermezzo: A Love Story* as if audiences didn't know already), though it fell short of psychological realism. The story, a simple one, deals with an aging, world-famous Swedish violinist, Howard, who finds himself emotionally enmeshed with a talented young pianist, Miss Bergman.

Edna Best and Ingrid Bergman

Ann Todd and Ingrid Bergman

Leslie Howard

Married and the father of two, Howard at first shies away from hurting his wife, Edna Best, who is still in love with him. He does not want his children's lives affected, but love proves too strong for him, and he and Miss Bergman, who also has her share of qualms, go off together. They embark on a concert tour of Europe with Bergman serving as Howard's accompanist. But when she realizes that Howard still yearns for his little daughter, and watches him playing wistfully with other people's children, she begins to ponder family friend John Halliday's admonition that happiness was never built on the unhappiness of others. And so, when she is offered a scholarship in Paris she writes Howard a parting note and tearfully departs their idyllic Mediterranean retreat.

Howard, who for his part had been pondering the philosophy that youthful romantic transports "come but once in one's life," declares to Halliday that Miss Bergman will always mean much to him, but by his manner indicates that the parting is all for the best. In time he returns to Sweden and after a near-fatal accident to his little girl, is reunited with the patient and forgiving Miss Best.

As in many other films of the romantic school, the logic leaves something to be desired, for often happiness *is* built on the unhappiness of others, the realities of human experience being what they are. And it is also an untruth that romantic love can come only once in one's life, and then at a relatively early age. This would seem to be an individual matter in actual experience—but of course such truths did not "play" well in romance-drenched 1939.

Despite psychological and motivational flaws, *Intermezzo* is a handsome and affecting picture. Its theme melody, also called *Intermezzo*, was popularized and became a tremendous hit. Miss Bergman projected a radiance all her own—wholesome, fresh-faced, clear-eyed, sincere—that stamped her an individual screen personality, a rare find. Howard was his usual polished, reflective self—the film was released just before Selznick's *Gone With the Wind*, in which he appeared to advantage as Ashley Wilkes —another of the Hamlet types this actor portrayed well. His reserved elegance and Miss Bergman's windswept insouciance complemented one another well. Ratoff kept the proceedings moving with the appropriate romantic tension. *Intermezzo* is one of its era's typical products, more tasteful than some, and very European in flavor.

Ingrid Bergman and Maria Flynn

Leslie Howard, Ann Todd and Edna Best

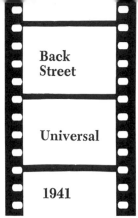

Back Street

Universal

1941

CREDITS: Directed by Robert Stevenson. Produced by Bruce Manning. Screenplay by Bruce Manning and Felix Jackson, based on the novel by Fannie Hurst. Photographed by William Daniels. Edited by Ted Kent.

OPENED at the Rivoli Theatre, New York, February 11, 1941. Running time: 89 minutes.

CAST: Charles Boyer (Walter Saxel); Margaret Sullavan (Ray Smith); Richard Carlson (Curt Stanton); Frank McHugh (Ed Porter); Frank Jenks (Harry); Tim Holt (Richard Saxel); Peggy Stewart (Freda Smith); Esther Dale (Mrs. Smith); Nell O'Day (Elizabeth Saxel); Kitty O'Neil (Mrs. Dilling); Nella Walker (Corinne Saxel); Cecil Cunningham (Mrs. Miller); Marjorie Gateson (Mrs. Adams); Dale Winter (Miss Evans).

Margaret Sullavan and Charles Boyer

Back Street, Fannie Hurst's novel, was a smash best-seller in 1930 and its perennially popular story was brought to the screen three times: in 1932 with Irene Dunne and John Boles, in 1941 with Margaret Sullavan and Charles Boyer, and in 1961 with Susan Hayward and John Gavin.

The Sullavan-Boyer version was easily the best of the three. There was a crude naivete about the 1932 picture, with less-than-solid production mounting, insufficient theme music to enhance the mood, and annoying anachronisms, to which some 1930s films were given—1932 hat styles in 1912 for instance. The 1961 edition with Hayward and Gavin was a glossy, foolish, high-style fashion-show extravaganza that displayed Ross Hunter's production ideas at their vulgar worst.

Which brings us to Sullavan and Boyer and their 1941 version. It was tragic drama at its most eloquent and appealing, exquisitely played by the principals and supporting players alike, directed with taste and restraint by English Robert Stevenson (his first Hollywood assignment) and well written by Bruce Manning and Felix Jackson, who caught the spirit of the original novel while editing and cinematizing the basic theme where needed.

The late Margaret Sullavan (1910-1960) was one

Richard Carlson and Margaret Sullavan

of the finest tragediennes the screen has ever known, and the 1941 *Back Street* was her masterpiece. An actress with a natural manner, a consummate sincerity, haunted eyes and a fetchingly husky voice, she was cited by the foremost stage and film critics of her day for what they described as her "radiance, forthright simplicity, wise reticence, honest feeling."

In *Back Street*, described by critic Bosley Crowther as "the quintessence of what is known as a 'woman's picture,'" she appeared to supreme advantage in the role of a self-sacrificing woman forced to live in the shadows of a man's life because of

his egoistic reluctance to sacrifice his career by divorcing his wife. She injected a realistic appeal into a part that in other hands might have degenerated into a neurotic, exhibitionistic bid for audience sympathy.

The 1941 film has been revived frequently on television in recent years and its freshness and emotional impact are undimmed. Charles Boyer, the distinguished French star, matched Miss Sullavan's interpretation with a polished delineation of Walter Saxel, the ambitious man who wanted to have it both ways, and though his is essentially the weaker role, he makes the most of it, pouring on the bed-

Charles Boyer and Margaret Sullavan

Frank Jenks, Margaret Sullavan and Frank McHugh

room-eyed Gallic charm that in that period made him irresistible to millions of women filmgoers.

The well-known story tells how Ray Smith, the girl from Cincinnati, meets traveling executive Saxel (Boyer) in 1900, they have a brief romance, terminated by his revelation that he is engaged to marry another; he changes his mind, calls her from the riverboat, where he has a parson ready, she rushes to join him but is waylayed by a crudely importunate suitor whom she has been avoiding. Boyer thinks she has stood him up and sails away. She arrives just in time to see the last of the boat down the river.

Five years later they meet again on a snowy New York street, and later at dinner he tells her how he had waited, of his plans to marry her, and is shocked by the surprised grief he sees in her face. In a handsomely composed scene, they stare at each other across the table, in their eyes the terrible sense of five years wasted.

Since he has married in the meantime, they must resort to subterfuges, and they find an apartment overlooking an inner court in a Greenwich Village street (a back street, of course) and for years he comes to visit her here when he can get away from family and career pressures.

The matter of his divorce comes up, but she realizes that he doesn't want to sacrifice the money and career that go with his well-connected marriage, and defers to his reluctance.

He goes to Europe with his family, another child is born in Spain, his postcards are few and far between. She has given up her job, and sits in the little apartment waiting for sign or word of him. Along comes handsome auto manufacturer Richard Carlson, whom she had known, and rejected, in Cincinnati, and he takes her to an auto race, introduces her to acquaintances—and she realizes how much mainstream life she has been cut off from. But once again she rejects his marriage proposal, and goes back to her lonely vigil.

Boyer returns from Europe, and she is shocked and grieved to learn that he has been back a week without calling her. "I'm no longer important in your life," she tells him, and without letting him know where she has gone, she returns to Cincinnati and wires Carlson that his marriage bid is accepted.

But Boyer follows her to Cincinnati, catches her as she is about to take the train to Detroit, Carlson, marriage and respectable safety—and persuades her to resume with him. "I couldn't go back to waiting, to loneliness, could I, Walter?" she implores as the train pulls out, but his look—Boyer was a master of the portentous look—gives her her answer.

Twenty-five years pass. It is now 1928. Boyer, his wife (Nella Walker), his son and daughter (Tim Holt and Nell O'Day) are about to board an ocean liner for France. He is a distinguished international banker on his way to the Geneva Conference. An aging, haunted-looking, heavily made-up woman follows up the gangplank at a distance, alone, and two

*Charles Boyer and
Margaret Sullavan*

women onlookers note her (she is Sullavan of course) and one comments to the other: "There goes one half of Walter Saxel's life—and here comes the other half." "Does the wife know?" the other gossip whispers. ''Heavens, no, Corinne thinks women like that only exist in French novels," she laughingly retorts. Which sets the 1928 scene and mood well enough.

In Paris there are complications, with Boyer's son and daughter staring at her with bleak hostility across a gaming table in a casino. Sullavan leaves immediately but the son (Holt) follows her to her Montmartre hideaway, where as usual she is joined by Boyer in his free time, and demands she get out of his father's world. "You're like a shadow over our lives," he tells her, adding that his sister is about to be married and gossip about her and his father may ruin the match.

Boyer arrives, is surprised to see his son, and tries to enlighten him on the twenty-five years of devotion he and Sullavan have known. As she stands sadly remembering, he details their years together but the boy only walks out saying they are both rotten and contemptible. Resignedly, they make plans for the next day, consoling each other as best they can. Boyer has lost an important assignment because of the gossip, and now his family has complicated their relationship, but he only asks, "Ray,

don't ever leave me," and she quietly replies, "I never will."

But the next morning finds him dying of a paralytic stroke, begging his reluctant son to put the telephone to his mouth and ear so that he can call the woman he loves. Over the phone she hears his dying gasps.

The boy goes to bring her a ticket back to America, but finds her ill and staring at a picture of his father. He goes to get a doctor, and she leans toward the photograph and asks, "I wonder what would have happened if . . ." Some excellent montage shots then show them being happily married on the riverboat, the music swells, the happy scene fades, and her head is lying by the picture. She, too, has passed on.

Back Street is a romantic picture of the first rank. Even in 1941 there was concern lest it seem dated, so the period covered was 1900 to 1928. Accepted as a period piece, and as an accurate reflection of the social conventions and cultural mores that restricted relationships in a certain time and social order, the film is a strengthful, dynamic depiction of the heart-wounds and soul-trials of an unconventional love. Moving and eloquent, with two superb stars and fine mounting, *Back Street* is a memorable experience for all who admire durable, well-crafted cinema.

That
Hamilton
Woman

Korda-

United
Artists

1941

CREDITS: Produced and directed by Alexander Korda. Original screenplay by Walter Reisch and R. C. Sherriff. Photographed by Rudolph Mate. Music by Miklos Rozsa. Edited by William Hornbeck.

OPENED at Radio City Music Hall, New York, April 3, 1941. Running time: 128 minutes.

CAST: Vivien Leigh (Emma, Lady Hamilton); Laurence Olivier (Lord Nelson); Alan Mowbray (Sir William Hamilton); Sara Allgood (Mrs. Cadogan-Lyon); Gladys Cooper (Lady Nelson); Henry Wilcoxon (Captain Hardy); Heather Angel (A Street Girl); Halliwell Hobbes (Reverend Nelson); Gilbert Emery (Lord Spencer); Miles Mander (Lord Keith); Ronald Sinclair (Josiah); Louis Alberni (King of Naples); Norma Drury (Queen of Naples); Olaf Hytten (Gavin); Juliette Compton (Lady Spencer); Guy Kingsford (Trowbridge).

Vivien Leigh and Laurence Olivier

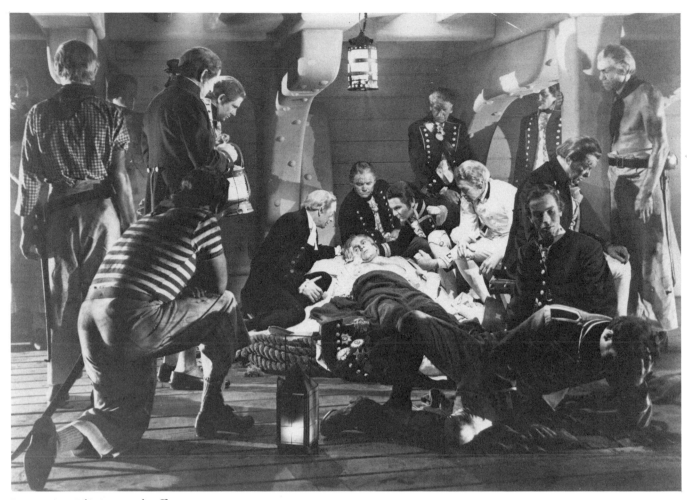

Laurence Olivier and officers

Vivien Leigh and Laurence Olivier

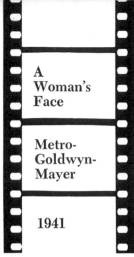

A Woman's Face

Metro-Goldwyn-Mayer

1941

CREDITS: Directed by George Cukor. Produced by Victor Saville. Screenplay by Donald Ogden Stewart. Based on the play *Il Etait Une Fois* by François de Croisset. Photographed by Robert Planck. Art Director by Cedric Gibbons. Music by Bronislau Kaper. Costumes by Adrian. Edited by Frank Sullivan.

OPENED at the Capitol Theatre, New York, May 15, 1941. Running time: 105 minutes.

CAST: Joan Crawford (Anna Holm); Melvyn Douglas (Dr. Gustaf Sergert); Conrad Veidt (Torsten Barring); Osa Massen (Vera Segert); Reginald Owen (Bernard Dalvik); Albert Basserman (Consul Magnus Barring); Marjorie Main (Emma Kristiansdotter); Donald Meek (Herman Rundvik); Connie Gilchrist (Christina Dalvik); Richard Nichols (Lars-Erik); Charles Quigley (Eric); Gwili Andre (Gusta); Clifford Brooke (Wickman); George Zucco (Defense Attorney); Henry Kolker (Judge); Robert Warwick (Associate Judge); Gilbert Emery (Associate Judge); Henry Daniell (Public Prosecutor); Sarah Padden (Police Matron); William Farnum (Court Attendant).

Joan Crawford and Melvyn Douglas

A Woman's Face was a product of Joan Crawford's later Metro-Goldwyn-Mayer period—the early 1940s era when she was struggling to supersede her clotheshorse image and be an actress. In retrospect, it is a much better film than it appeared at the time of its 1941 release, and with George Cukor to guide her, Miss Crawford contributed one of her more sensitive and trenchant performances. Two years before Cukor had disciplined her into a striking performance in *The Women*, followed by a commend-able stint in *Susan And God*. By 1941 Miss Crawford was anxiously seeking to continue her upward progress as a serious actress, and a remake of *A Woman's Face*, a film Ingrid Bergman had made in Sweden in the 1930s, seemed the right move.

Donald Ogden Stewart constructed a carefully wrought, tasteful and literate screen treatment from the play *Il Etait Une Fois* by Francois Croisset. The film was well mounted, with Bronislau Kaper's evocative music not the least of its attractions, and

Joan Crawford, Albert Bassermann and Marjorie Main

Melvyn Douglas and Joan Crawford

Reginald Owen, Joan Crawford,
Connie Gilchrist and Donald Meek

in it Miss Crawford gave a performance that was her best of the MGM period. From 1941 to 1943 she was to know more career discouragements ("They laughed when I asked to do *Madame Curie* and *Random Harvest*," she later reminisced), but her final MGM years were to prove the darkness before the dawn of a fresh career at Warner's and her Academy Award (for 1945's *Mildred Pierce*).

Joan Crawford's *A Woman's Face* is a softer, more romantic, more delicately drawn rendition of the character and basic story than is Ingrid Bergman's, which tends more toward the naturalistic. Castigated in its time as overly sentimental and contrived, and an uneasy blend of the emotional and the melodramatic, the Crawford version is gaining increased respect and qualifies today as a fine example of the romantic school.

The plot recounts how Anna Holm (Miss Crawford), horribly scarred in childhood on one side of her face, turned to an embittered and lonely life in Stockholm. Feeling that the world rejects her because of her ugliness, she has taken to leading a gang of blackmailers. At a roadhouse she owns, she encounters a nobleman, Torsten Barring (Conrad Veidt) who is embittered for his own reasons: his small nephew, Lars Eric (Richard Nichols) by his mere existence threatens his inheritance from his relative, Consul Magnus Barring (Albert Basserman). Meanwhile Anna has been blackmailing the wife (Osa Massen) of plastic surgeon Melvyn Douglas, who has written indiscreet love letters.

Through an accident, Anna encounters the surgeon, who persuades her to undergo an operation. With her beauty restored, she goes to Barring, with whom she has fallen in love, and he cynically uses her to further his plan: the murder of his young nephew. Anna goes as a governess to the Barring household but her personality has changed and she finds she cannot further the plot. Barring follows and tries to force her hand, but is killed by Anna when he drives off with the child during a sleighing party. The film begins and ends with Anna's trial, at which she is eventually exonerated after the discovery of a letter she had written warning the consul.

There are many romantically compelling scenes, especially in the film's first half: Anna playing Chopin for Barring soon after their initial meeting, Anna's visit to the philandering young wife at which they discuss love and the girl taunts her for her scarred face, her walk through the park after her operation—when she persists in pulling her hat down over the once-scarred side of her face, a characteristic gesture born of long defensive habit, a little boy's admiring smile gives her a finally liberated self-image and she takes off the hat and continues joyfully through the park with her hair blowing in the wind, her first visit to Barring after the surgery, and their mutual delight in the transformation.

The second half of *A Woman's Face* gets down to the business of melodrama but there are still many compelling scenes. The role of the plastic surgeon, which was not accented romantically in the Swedish version, in the hands of Melvyn Douglas, the favorite leading man of Garbo, Crawford, Shearer, and others, becomes a springboard for the love relationship between him and Miss Crawford, especially toward the end, when he finally realizes that her character has been transformed for the better, along with her face.

The film is replete with fine performances, especially that of Conrad Veidt, who gets many subtle nuances into the character and personality of the selfish, conniving Torsten Barring.

An authentically romantic film, for all its occasional biting cynicism and strong melodrama, *A Woman's Face* is a tour de force for one of Hollywood's high priestesses of romance at her MGM zenith—a harbinger of the great things to come at Warners'.

Conrad Veidt and Joan Crawford

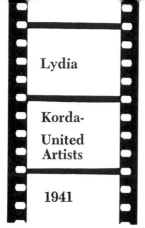

Lydia

Korda-United Artists

1941

CREDITS: Directed by Julien Duvivier. Produced by Alexander Korda. Screenplay by Ben Hecht and Samuel Hoffenstein. Based on a story by Julien Duvivier and L. Bush-Fekete. Production designed by Vincent Korda. Photographed by Lee Garmes. Music by Miklos Rozsa. Associate Art Director, Jack Okie. Interior settings by Julie Heron. Special effects by Lawrence Butler. Costumes by Marcel Vertes and Walter Plunkett. Edited by William Hornbeck.

OPENED at Radio City Music Hall, New York, September 18, 1941. Running time: 103 minutes.

CAST: Merle Oberon (Lydia MacMillan); Edna May Oliver (Granny); Alan Marshall (Richard Mason); Joseph Cotten (Michael Fitzpatrick); Hans Yaray (Frank Andre); George Reeves (Bob Willard); John Halliday (Fitzpatrick the Butler); Sara Allgood (Johnny's Mother); Billy Ray (Johnny); Frank Conlon (Old Ned).

Merle Oberon and Alan Marshall

Lydia MacMillan, the heroine of Julien Duvivier's nostalgic love story, is said to be like "all women— wise and foolish, clever and absurd, good and bad." As the talented and beautiful Merle Oberon plays her in this handsomely mounted Alexander Korda production, she is also displayed as romantic and self-destructive, and not a little self-deluding.

But then how could Lydia help being what she was, with that salty, shrewd old New England grandmother (Edna May Oliver in one of her final, and best, performances) egging her on to be an individualist, and heady romances with four young men, circa 1897, three of whom love her unrequitedly and one of whom *she* loves unrequitedly.

Coming as she does from one of the best families, with money too, she has something of a New England conscience, and when her romantic life comes a cropper, Lydia spends the next forty years becoming a sort of Eleanor Roosevelt (or is it Mary Baker Eddy) of the blind, endowing homes for sightless children and working among the bereft and afflicted.

Fine, but what of the man who got away?

He is, of course, handsome and charming Alan Marshall, who in the early 1940s was enjoying a not-inconsiderable *homme fatal* vogue that speedily assigned Mr. John Boles to has-been status. Richard Mason (Marshall) is, unfortunately for Lydia, a love-em-leave-em type, and after taking her on a snow-steeped wintry idyll in her family lodge off the Maine

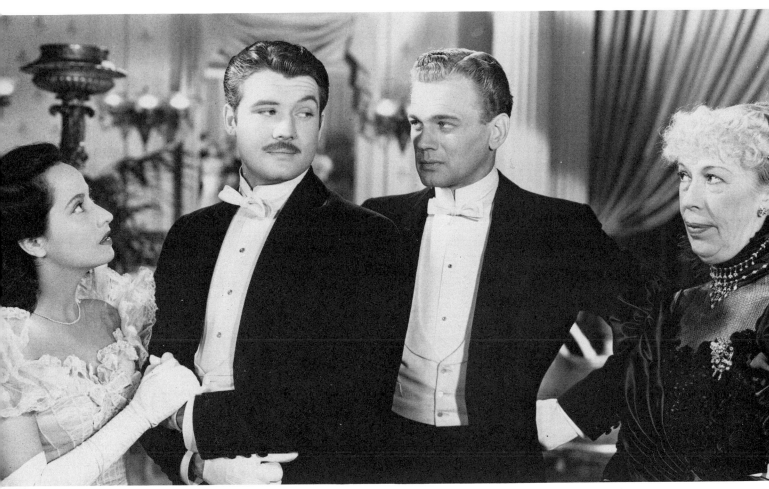

Merle Oberon, George Reeves, Joseph Cotten and Edna May Oliver

coast, where for a few days she knows the most sublime happiness of her life, he writes her that he has a romantic entanglement elsewhere, must go back to wherever he came from to straighten it out, and that he will then return to be hers forever. Lydia, being romantically naive, believes every word of it, and goes on carrying the torch for the next four decades, and without a word from her onetime love.

So much for him. Her other three loves comprise George Reeves, a noodle-headed football player who talks her into an elopement but disillusions her, luckily before the knot is tied, with his heavy drinking and coltish behavior. Then there's Hans Yaray, a blind musician who composes music inspired by his love for Lydia, and whom she encounters during her excursions among the blind. She almost gets to the starting post with *this* young man (compassion, maternalism, protectiveness—call it what you will) but back from the Spanish War comes Doctor Michael Fitzpatrick (Joe Cotten straight from his *Citizen Kane* triumph) and then she decides she might love *him*. Michael, it seems, is something of a "good old Charlie" type who has stood by patiently since his days as the butler's son in Lydia's family mansion. He has been functioning, with Fido-like forebearance, as her good friend and

Merle Oberon, Edna May Oliver and Joseph Cotten

95

Merle Oberon and Edna May Oliver

Merle Oberon and George Reeves

shoulder-to-cry-on for longer than he cares to remember, but he too is left in the lurch, as Lydia, deciding once and for all that Richard, the man who loved and left, is her only true love, retires into eminent reclusiveness.

Many years later, she and Michael meet at the dedication of one of her institutions for children, and he arranges a strange little party, with all her old loves present. There's Reeves, now old and portly, and Yaray, wispy and fragile, and of course Michael himself. Though all are now in their sixties, he still hasn't given up hope of winning Lydia.

And then a fourth guest, at Michael's express invitation, makes an appearance. It is the long-lost Mr. Marshall, of course, and he is white-haired and bearded, and has no idea why he is there. He is introduced to Lydia, and fails to remember her or their previous encounter forty-odd years before.

Finally brought conclusively down to the realities of life and love as they actually exist, and not as her romantic dreams would have them, the aged Lydia dodders out to the terrace—followed by the ever-faithful, ever-loving Michael, who tells the others that while Richard didn't remember her, *he* would know her no matter how many years had

Merle Oberon and George Reeves

passed. Bereft of illusions, but resting in Michael's love, which she now recognizes as mature and enduring, Lydia accepts the inevitable philosophically, with a wry smile lighting up her wrinkles and glazing old eyes. ,

Duvivier, who directed the famed French film, *Un Carnet du Bal*, which boasted a somewhat similar plot (a woman recalls the boys she knew at her first ball), gave *Lydia* a considerable amount of continental verve and nostalgic eclat. Lee Garmes photographed Oberon and company to flattering effect (though the lovely Merle was *not* believable as an old lady) and Miklos Rozsa produced memorable melodies during the Maine-coast-idyll sequences between Richard and Lydia—and wherever else they were needed, for that matter. Ben Hecht's and Samuel Hoffenstein's screenplay caught the nuances of aristocratic speech and manners of the late 1890s, and the period atmosphere in general is especially commendable.

For all its wry attitude toward romantic love, and its deification of the loyal and true friend, *Lydia* is so drenched, from start to finish, with romantic atmosphere that it qualifies for the genre hands-down.

Alan Marshall, Merle Oberon and Joseph Cotten

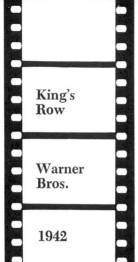

King's Row

Warner Bros.

1942

CREDITS: Directed by Sam Wood. Associate Producer, David Lewis. Screenplay by Casey Robinson. Based on the novel by Henry Bellamann. Photographed by James Wong Howe. Music by Erich Wolfgang Korngold. Art Direction by Carl Jules Weyl. Edited by Ralph Dawson.

OPENED at the Astor Theatre, New York, February 2, 1942. Running time: 127 minutes.

CAST: Ann Sheridan (Randy Monaghan); Robert Cummings (Parris Mitchell); Ronald Reagan (Drake McHugh); Betty Field (Cassandra Tower); Charles Coburn (Dr. Henry Gordon); Claude Rains (Dr. Alexander Tower); Judith Anderson (Mrs. Harriet Gordon); Nancy Coleman (Louise Gordon); Maria Ouspenskaya (Madame Von Elm); Harry Davenport (Colonel Skeffington); Kaaren Verne (Elise Sandor); Ernest Cossart (Pa Monaghan); Scotty Beckett (Parris Mitchell as a boy); Douglas Wheat (Drake McHugh as a boy); Mary Thomas (Cassandra Tower as a girl); Ann Todd (Randy Monaghan as a girl); Joan Duval (Louise Gordon as a girl); Pat Moriarty (Tad Monaghan); Ilka Gruning (Anna).

Robert Cummings and Ann Sheridan

King's Row is the romance of a small Midwestern town circa 1900—and a grim, grotesque romance it is. Sam Wood was assigned by the Warners to direct it, possibly because he had guided Thornton Wilder's *Our Town* to the cinema two years before. Compared to *King's Row*, *Our Town* is an affirmative, life-loving, joyous romp, as Wood presently discovered—and perhaps in time he wished he had never undertaken the Warner assignment.

For the people who first thrived in Henry Bellamann's stark gothic exercise in small-town grotesquerie were so minutely drawn, and so sharply observed in psychological terms, that their tran-

Ann Sheridan and Ronald Reagan

Ronald Reagan (at left); Robert Cummings (at right)

scription to the screen—or at least as many of them as a 127-minute running time could accommodate—seemed denuding, and an oversimplifying sketching-out, in quick, perfunctory strokes, of characters of considerable complexity and Janus-faced unpredictability.

Scripter Casey Robinson, an old hand at translating in screen terms the often-turgid and obscure products of other mediums, waded through the Bellamann novel and extracted what he considered the high spots, and he is not greatly to be blamed for the watering-down of the twisted psychodynamics and unhealthy perversities of the Kings-Rowites, some of whom were pretty strong stuff for the 1942 cinema.

Wood directed, however, with precision and dispatch, Robinson's script kept the screen characters hurrying through well staged, highly theatricalized scenes and situations, and talented musician Erich Wolfgang Korngold really saved the day with some passionately evocative music filled with emotional alarums and stirring crescendoes.

King's Row also contained Robert Cummings's best alltime performance. A sensitive actor, not usually cast wisely, he seemed to empathize deeply with the character of Parris Mitchell, the sensitive, introspective boy who lives with his relative and mentor, Madame Von Elm, and who falls in love with demented Cassandra Tower (Betty Field) the daughter of Dr. Alexander Tower (Claude Rains), who is tutoring Parris in medicine preparatory to college studies. Dr. Tower eventually kills Cassandra,

Ann Sheridan and Ronald Reagan

Ronald Reagan, Ernest Cossart and Ann Sheridan

presumably to save her from a darker fate, her mental aberration being incurable, and then kills himself, with both deaths leaving the impressionable Parris bereft.

Ronald Reagan also appeared to advantage as Drake McHugh, the town sport ("stud" would have been the word today), who forms a friendship with Parris despite the difference in temperament and mental endowment. He is loved by Randy Monaghan (Ann Sheridan) the daughter of an Irish railroad worker, who has known him and Parris from childhood. When Dr. Henry Gordon (Charles Coburn) begins to get the idea, however, that there has been monkey-business between the rakish McHugh and his daughter Louise (Nancy Coleman) he takes diabolical revenge by amputating both of Drake's legs after a fluke accident in which he had been knocked cold but had *not* sustained serious injuries.

But before this shattering event, Parris has mooned and introspected, romanced Cassandra, grieved over her death, gone to Vienna to become a doctor, and returned to King's Row in time to clean up, with his idealism and good will, some of the messes he finds.

For instance, when Parris learns from Louise of her father's horrible deed, he finds it necessary to tell Randy, who has taken Drake into her home. Drake, who wakes up one morning in horror to ask the famous question "Where's the rest of me?!"—a title used by the later Governor Ronald Reagan of California for his autobiography—has gone into a period of melancholia and self-disgust and Randy despairs of raising his spirits. Psychiatrist Parris decides the only answer is to tell his friend the truth —that his legs had been cut off without reason, and because of the doctor's vengeful nature—and challenges him to rise above it all. Drake, being a young man of some spirit, proceeds to do just that, to the enormous relief of Parris and Randy, the two people who love him most.

Whereupon Parris rushes off to his new love, Elise Sandor (Kaaren Verne). This recital of the bare bones of the plot may leave some thinking that the picture is a lot sillier than it really is. Actually, the intensely romantic ambience, the sincere acting, Korngold's music, Wood's sensitive direction, and the fine acting of Cummings; Rains, Sheridan and Reagan (with Betty Field as the unfortunate Cassandra making her usual distinctive contribution) lift the picture to the level of authentic romance. There is a strange haunting power to it, a sense of the unseen and the unspoken, a spiritual force all the more potent for being indefinable.

But after guiding the gentle steed *Our Town*, Wood must have felt here that he was breaking in a Bellamann bronco.

Now, Voyager

Warner Bros.

1942

CREDITS: Directed by Irving Rapper. Produced by Hal B. Wallis. Screenplay by Casey Robinson. Based on the novel by Olive Higgins Prouty. Photographed by Sol Polito. Music by Max Steiner. Musical director by Leo F. Forbstein. Art Direction by Robert Haas. Edited by Warren Low.

OPENED at the Hollywood Theatre, New York, October 22, 1942. Running time: 118 minutes.

CAST: Bette Davis (Charlotte Vale); Paul Henreid (Jerry Durrance); Claude Rains (Dr. Jaquith); Gladys Cooper (Mrs. Henry Windle Vale); Bonita Granville (June Vale); Ilka Chase (Lisa Vale); John Loder (Elliott Livingston); Lee Patrick (Deb McIntyre); Franklin Pangborn (Mr. Thompson); Katherine Alexander (Miss Trask); James Rennie (Frank McIntyre); Mary Wickes (Dora Pickford); Janis Wilson (Tina Durrance); Michael Ames (Dr. Dan Regan); Charles Drake (Leslie Trotter); Frank Puglia (Manoel); David Clyde (William).

Bette Davis, Bonita Granville, Ilka Chase, and others

Bette Davis

"The Untold Want, By Life Nor Land Ne'er Granted, Now Voyager, Sail Thou Forth to Seek and Find," wrote the eloquent Walt Whitman in his *Leaves of Grass*, and the thought, and message—were eloquently and movingly illustrated in one of Bette Davis's finest romantic dramas, appropriately titled, *Now, Voyager*.

From the moment the exciting and dynamic Warner trademark fanfare is heard over the Warner silver shield (with signature music composed by Max Steiner and in use since 1937) there is a feeling of excitement and glamorous portent, in this instance amply justified by what ensues, and when the credit cards announce the principals, against the background drawing of a great ship, one of Max Steiner's finest, most lyric scores (for which he won the 1942 Oscar, his second) grips the emotions and generates spiritual tension.

And tension is the word for it, as Bette Davis acts her heart out, and in her most passionate, intense style, as Charlotte Vale, the ugly duckling misfit of a stuffy Boston "first family" who, from their behavior, speak neither to the Cabots, Lowells nor God Himself. And there is Gladys Cooper, the domineering, subtly sadistic matriarch of the clan, demanding that Charlotte obey her every wish, wear what she chooses, read what she chooses. Overweight, dressed in dowdy dresses, wearing what her mother dubs "sensible" shoes, her eyes shielded in glasses that give her the look of a psyched-out squirrel, this pathetic case retreats to her room at the top of the great Boston mansion, where she drinks forbidden sherry, smokes forbidden cigarettes, and carves ivory boxes that no one but herself sees.

And then there are her patronizing relatives who whisper, "Poor Charlotte . . ." Her cruel, bitchy young niece, Bonita Granville, ridicules her constantly. The servants shake their heads over it all. And kindly sister-in-law Ilka Chase brings to the great mansion the psychiatrist, Claude Rains, who sets in motion this ugly duckling's eventual metamorphosis into a swan of swans.

But first she must undergo considerable travail, lose twenty-five pounds, have a fancy nervous breakdown, complete with nonstop crying jags, stop being what Dr. Jaquith (Rains) calls a creature "with a hidebound New England conscience." All conspire to keep her away from the dragon on Boston's Marlborough Street until the transformation is complete. She is sent off on a cruise to South America, made-up to the nines, dolled up in borrowed clothing from which she has forgotten to take the notes and tags ("This is bound to look good—it will do things for you, etc.") Indeed, now that she is slim and well-groomed, well-coiffed and well-dressed, she has become quite a handsome thing indeed—but that matter of wounded self-image and truncated self-confidence must be taken care of—and handsome Paul Henreid, a fellow passenger on the great ship, is just the man for the job.

Paul Henreid and Bette Davis

It seems Henreid, too, is unhappy, being married to a shrew with hypochrondriac leanings whom he no longer loves, and he and Davis comfort each other. They wind up together in a Brazilian cabin where "he gave me something warm to drink, and because of the drink I lost my inhibitions," and then it's a series of passionate love scenes, and the final parting when both realize they must go home—he to the wife he cannot in all conscience desert, and she to the lion's cage in Beantown. But to make a long and eloquent story short, as she later tells him, "When you told me that you loved me, I was so proud; I could have walked into a den of lions; in fact I did, and the lion didn't hurt me."

And so, armed with the memory of loving and being loved truly and completely, a new, sleek, attractive, confident Davis returns to Boston, puts the old lady in her place, wins her relatives' respect, becomes something of a social light and lands herself an attractive widower (John Loder). However,

Bette Davis and Paul Henreid

Bette Davis

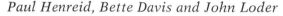

Paul Henreid, Bette Davis and John Loder

Henreid appears in Boston on an engineering assignment, they meet briefly and part again, and she realizes that she can only be happy in marriage with someone she loves. She breaks the engagement to the aristocrat, quarrels with her mother over it, the old lady dies of shock, and then it's off to Doctor Jaquith's sanitarium *again*.

But while there she meets Henreid's daughter Tina, who is much like herself at that age, blighted, wounded, misanthropic—and so loses herself in bringing happiness and health to the child that she forgets to have a nervous breakdown. In a resolution that is short on sense but long on emotional appeal, she and Henreid agree that Tina is "their" child, and that they must sacrifice their mutual passion in a platonic partnership. Again he goes back to his wife and she is left with the child.

Such is the story. Bette Davis has said she had to fight hard to get this plum (the Warners wanted Irene Dunne) "just as I always had to fight to get anything good." One Warner producer told her he couldn't stand the kind of things she wanted to do in pictures but as long as they made money he didn't object. She meddled in everything, proved her artistry and taste were not confined to acting. She didn't like some of the script so restored portions of the Prouty novel she thought apposite. "If meddling was producing, I'd been a producer for years," she later said.

Now, Voyager, and Bette Davis as its centerpiece, were ahead of their time, for in 1942 such piercing insights into the human condition and the deep recesses of the human heart were considered revolutionary. To dress unattractively and dare to suggest that there are a lot of frustrated frumps and harried harridans in the world was considered heretically antithetical to the Merle Oberon-style glamour that was being busily purveyed, and Miss Davis gets a plus for this brand of pioneering as she does for many other cinematic advances she insisted on and promoted.

Sol Polito's photography, Max Steiner's music, and Bette Davis's eloquent acting were never teamed to better effect than in one fascinating scene: she is telling psychiatrist Rains, early in the picture, of her difficult past. She flips before him the pages of an old photo album. "Look," she says, tense and wild-eyed, "You wouldn't have known me then— I was twenty then" and the pages flip back-back-back and suddenly, to the swelling chords of a Steiner alarum, she is discovered kissing handsome ship's officer Charles Drake on a sunswept deck. This kind of montage magic helped make the picture, but its fine acting, solid dramatic content, positive philosophy, and buoyant spiritual élan will keep *Now, Voyager* high on the list of Hollywood's great romantic films for all time to come.

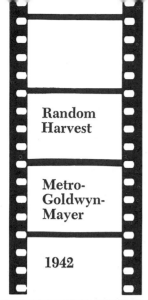

Random Harvest

Metro-Goldwyn-Mayer

1942

CREDITS: Directed by Mervyn Le Roy. Produced by Sidney Franklin. Adapted for the screen by Claudine West, George Froeschel and Arthur Wimperis from the novel of the same name by James Hilton. Photographed by Joseph Ruttenberg. Edited by Harold F. Kress.

OPENED at Radio City Music Hall, New York, December 17, 1942. Running time: 125 minutes.

CAST: Ronald Colman (Charles Rainier); Greer Garson (Paula); Philip Dorn (Doctor Jonathan Benet); Susan Peters (Kitty); Henry Travers (Doctor Sims); Reginald Owen ("Biffer"); Bramwell Fletcher (Harrison); Rhys Williams (Sam); Una O'Connor (Tobacconist); Charles Waldron (Mr. Lloyd); Elizabeth Risdon (Mrs. Lloyd); Melville Cooper (George); Margaret Wycherly (Mrs. Deventer); Aubrey Mather (Sheldon); Arthur Margetson (Chetwynd); Alan Napier (Julian); Jill Esmond (Lydia); Marta Linden (Jill); Ann Richards (Bridget); Norma Varden (Julia); David Cavendish (Henry Chilcet); Ivan Simpson (The Vicar); Marie de Becher (The Vicar's Wife).

Greer Garson and Ronald Colman

Amnesia has given occasion for many a romantic treatment on stage, screen, television and in literature, and one of the better examples came in 1942 with the release of MGM's *Random Harvest*. Based on a 1940 James Hilton novel, it displayed Ronald Colman and Greer Garson at their most attractive and persuasive. Mr. Colman, just turned fifty, was getting on for a romantic lead and might have lent his role more credibility had he been fifteen or even ten years younger; nonetheless, he turned in a performance replete with all the expected Colman charm and polish.

Miss Garson, on the wave of her signal triumph in *Mrs. Miniver*, in which she had portrayed an English matron enduring heroically the vicissitudes of World War II (it was to win her the 1942 Academy

Greer Garson and Philip Dorn

Award), gave to her *Random Harvest* portrayal a characteristic vibrancy.

Produced by Sidney Franklin, who was noted for his impeccable taste, and adapted with considerable literacy by scenarists Claudine West, George Froeschel and Arthur Wimperis, the story dealt with one Charles Rainier (Colman), an Englishman of wealth and social standing, who goes as an officer to World War I, loses his memory in action, develops a speech block, finds himself in an asylum as a mental case, and wanders off the grounds during a frenetic celebration of Armistice Day.

He becomes involved with a music hall entertainer, Paula (Miss Garson), who takes the forlorn man under her wing, restores his confidence, teaches him to speak normally again, and helps him regain his interest in the world and his trust in people. But he continues to recall nothing prior to that day in 1917 when disaster struck on the battleground in France.

Their mutual love grows, they marry, have a child, and Colman develops writing ambitions. One day he goes into town to negotiate the sale of a story he has written, and is struck by a taxi. The shock restores his pre-1917 memory of events —and destroys his recollection of everything that has happened since. He returns to his prominent family near London, resumes his career as an industrialist —and continues to puzzle over the three-year "lost period" in his life. While he muses, he is courted by the smitten Susan Peters, but finds that his emotions are strangely vacant and that he is searching for something lost, something incomplete, he knows not what.

Miss Garson, grief-stricken when he fails to return home, eventually finds him again—but he doesn't remember her, and she decides that if he cannot renew his love for her, as well as his memory, by his own volition, there is no use briefing him on the past. She goes to work as his assistant, and becomes indispensable to him. Though he isn't in love with her—or more accurately, doesn't remember being so—he asks her to marry him. She agrees, and ever watchful, ever hopeful, she searches for signs that he is recalling matters concerning that 1917–1920 period.

His essential coldness, however polite, and the vacancy in his eyes, desolate her, and she almost

Susan Peters and Ronald Colman

*Greer Garson and
Ronald Colman*

gives up. But through still another fluke, his memory comes back bit by bit, and he traces his way eventually to the cottage where they had once known a short-lived happiness. Miss Garson has followed him there, drawing hope from each clue he unravels, and calls out "Smitty!" the name under which she had known him during their three-year idyll. He recognizes her at last, all his old love for her comes back with his clearing mind—and permanent happiness is presaged for them.

That is the story, and romantic it was—and just the ticket for 1942–43 audiences confronted daily with tragic war news. Many viewing it in that era had suffered personal tragedies due to the times and the great conflict raging—and its sympathetic treat-

ment, the restrained, eloquent performances of the principals and supporting cast, the excellent mounting and direction by Mervyn LeRoy made *Random Harvest* a popular favorite.

True, in some aspects the picture defies the rules of logic. The coincidences and happenstances are worked up too patly, the psychology is shaky, and the MGM music department poured on the molten melodic fudge so determinedly that at times the dialogue was drowned out—a frequent drawback in MGM dramas of the period. But with suave, sensitive Ronald Colman and tender, womanly Greer Garson up front, and a story that purged the emotions while vitiating abstract analysis, who was there to quibble? Few did.

A Song to Remember

Columbia

1945

CREDITS: Directed by Charles Vidor. Produced by Sidney Buchman. Screenplay by Sidney Buchman, adapted from a story by Ernst Marischka. Recordings by Jose Iturbi. Color by Technicolor. Musical Supervision, Mario Silva. Musical Director, M. W. Stoloff. Photographed by Tony Gaudio and Allen M. Davey. Art Direction by Lionel Banks, Van Nest Polglase. Edited by Charles Nelson. Technicolor Consultant, Natalie Kalmus.

OPENED at Radio City Music Hall, New York, January 25, 1945. Running time: 120 minutes.

CAST: Paul Muni (Professor Joseph Elsner); Merle Oberon (George Sand); Cornel Wilde (Frederic Chopin); Stephen Bekassy (Franz Liszt); Nina Foch (Constantia); George Coulouris (Louis Pleyel); Sig Arno (Henry Dupont); Howard Freeman (Kalkbrenner); George Macready (Alfred de Musset); Claire Du Brey (Madame Mercier); Frank Puglia (Monsieur Jollet); Fern Emmett (Madame Lambert); Sybil Merritt (Isabelle Chopin).

Merle Oberon

A handsome Technicolor extravaganza—that is the word for it—burst on the nation's screens in early 1945, and though laid supposedly in the Paris of the 1830s and 1840s, *A Song to Remember*, a largely fictionized version of the life of Frederic Chopin, was replete with as much mid-1940s Hollywood gloss, decor, mounting and lavish montage as could be summoned—indeed beyond the call of duty.

Directed by Charles Vidor with all the sweep and emotional vitality for which he was noted, and produced by Sidney Buchman from a screenplay by Buchman adapted from a story by Ernst Marischka, it showcased a highly mannered, almost grotesquely attitudinizing Paul Muni, tearing his scenes to tat-

ters as Professor Joseph Elsner, Chopin's teacher and mentor, a decadently, lush, piercingly intense Merle Oberon as the flamboyant George Sand, the eccentric novelist who sported men's clothes, lived life according to her own special rules, and flaunted a legion of lovers, and (walking humbly in such company) Cornel Wilde as an elegantly anemic, highly suggestible, tormentedly brooding, and on occasion posturing, Frederic Chopin.

The basic facts of Chopin's life were twisted, indeed distorted by a freewheeling screenplay. Among the inaccuracies: Chopin, though sympathetic to Polish nationalism, was never an active Polish revolutionist, nor did he concretely aid the cause. Elsner did not accompany Chopin to Paris from Poland, nor did he ever engage in a duel of wits with George Sand for control of Chopin's life and aims; Constantia, the character played by Nina Foch, never went to Paris to plead with Chopin to help his fellow Poles in their struggle against Czarist rule, Elsner and Sand never reflected—nor influenced—Chopin's musical style to the degree implied in the film, which tries to apply relatively cut-and-dried, black-and-white motivations for his dreamy romantic musical images (allegedly Sand-influenced) as against his militaristic, patriotic, more brittle melodies, which the movie implies were brought about by Elsner's insistence that he be patriotically concerned.

Nor in actual fact did Chopin, his health failing, embark on a suicidal tour of Europe that eventually killed him. In fact, London was Chopin's only concertizing stop-over, with Paris, Nohant and Majorca his main bases for the short thirty-nine years of his life.

Having taken due note of all this, it is only fair to state that if one is willing to surrender to the gorgeous romanticism of the doings, and if one approaches *A Song to Remember* as a fictionalized tale about a nineteenth century composer who wrote beautiful, melodic, enchanting piano music, who loved the eccentric but mesmeric Sand, wanted to help his fellow Poles in the effort, proved ungrateful to Elsner, who had made his Paris career possible, then one is confronted with an authentically romantic sequence of events, filled to the brim with conflict (especially between Sand and Elsner);

George Macready and Merle Oberon

Cornel Wilde playing at salon

rousing, lightning-style emotional scenes courtesy of Miss Oberon, who was never more forceful and electric than in this, and the highly individual and always fascinating thespian pyrotechnics of Paul Muni, who when he was good was very very good and when he was bad was—even more fascinating. Here he pours it on excessively, compelling, nonetheless, admiration for his minutely observed characterization.

Miss Oberon, who seems to have fully understood the character of the tempestuous George Sand, or at least the character presented her by scripter Buchman, wears gorgeous gowns, strikingly flamboyant male attire, swaggers hither and thither with fetching éclat, waxes feline when occasion demands, and outplays Muni in some tense confrontation scenes as they struggle for Wilde's attention and fealty.

When the languid but determined Wilde, guilt-ridden by his neglect of his countrymen's interests, decides to embark on the concert tour that will raise money for "the cause," Miss Oberon works herself into a fine lather, tells her boy off in fierce style, and rattles off an arresting monologue about the bitternesses and sorrows in her past that had hardened her resolve to meet men on equal terms and defy the world with her individualism—all of which would do credit to Miss Bette Davis at her most trenchant, though we hasten to add that Miss Oberon is very much an original.

Vidor keeps tight control over the material, and sends the flamboyant doings in constant motion—the 120 minutes fly by. Fine characterizations are contributed by Stephen Bekassy as Franz Liszt, George Coulouris as music publisher Louis Pleyel, and George Macready as Alfred de Musset, one of the more conspicuous lovers of Sand.

Atmospherically it is first-rate. In the Majorca scenes, a failing Wilde, his condition worsened by the climate, tinkles away at his piano while the tigress Oberon, quill pen poised like a dagger over her manuscript paper, listens intently and schemes to keep him hers forever. And when Wilde collapses after the concert tour, Muni goes to a haughty, icy Oberon who is posing unconcernedly for a Delacroix painting, to plead with her to pay a deathbed visit to the man who had rejected her for patriotic pursuits, she informs him with clipped dispatch that she certainly has no place at such a scene and asks Muni if he is satisfied to have destroyed so unique a talent as Chopin's. He slinks out and Merle the Imperious, her oriental-slanted eyes like slits, hisses "Continue, Mr. Delacroix!"

Some two dozen Chopin compositions grace the soundtrack courtesy of pianist Jose Iturbi, and Cornel Wilde obviously did his homework, for his playing looks realistic enough. He peregrinates through lavish Paris salons, music-publishing houses, taverns, eateries, soirées, and Sand's retreats in France and elsewhere with a puppyish insouciance

Cornel Wilde, Stephen Bekassy, Merle Oberon, George Macready and Paul Muni

Merle Oberon, Cornel Wilde, Paul Muni, George Coulouris and Howard Freeman

Paul Muni and Cornel Wilde

increasingly dulled by his character's declining health and spirits, and he winds up a pinch-faced, languorous fellow indeed. And at the end he dies in fine style in an enormous bed in an enormous room while Muni, Nina Foch and other faithful souls look on in muted sorrow and Stephen Bekassy, as Liszt, plays Chopin's "Nocturne in C Minor" in a neighboring room.

If taken as an essentially fictional work, *A Song to Remember* is lush romanticism at its most typical, and highly entertaining to boot. Music purists and nitpicking historians may be rendered unhappy with it—in fact, they were and are—but since 1945, audiences in love with love and empathetic with Chopin's melodic inspirations have been eating it up.

111

The
Enchanted
Cottage

RKO-
Radio

1945

CREDITS: Directed by John Cromwell. Produced by Harriet Parsons. Screenplay by De Witt Bodeen and Herman J. Mankiewicz, based on the play by Sir Arthur Wing Pinero. Photographed by Ted Tetzlaff. Art direction by Albert S. D'Agostino and Carroll Clark. Set decorations by Darrell Silvera and Harley Miller. Music by Roy Webb. Musical Direction by C. Bakaleinikoff. Assistant Director, Fred Fleck. Edited by Joseph Noriega. Recorded by Richard Van Hessen.

OPENED at the Astor Theatre, New York, April 27, 1945. Running time: 92 minutes.

CAST: Dorothy McGuire (Laura); Robert Young (Oliver); Herbert Marshall (John Hillgrave); Mildred Natwick (Abigail Minnett); Spring Byington (Violet Price); Richard Gaines (Frederick); Hillary Brooke (Beatrice); Alec Englander (Danny); Mary Worth (Mrs. Stanton); Josephine Whittell (Canteen Manager); Robert Clarke (Marine); Eden Nicholas (Soldier).

Robert Young and Dorothy McGuire

Sir Arthur Wing Pinero's *The Enchanted Cottage* was one of the most tender and sensitive of plays, greatly loved in its time. It was later made as a popular silent film with Richard Barthelmess and May McAvoy. In 1945, as a sound film, it won a cordial reception, coming as it did near the close of a disastrous war which had brought untold suffering to many millions. The basic story has strong heart appeal, even to this day, as an allegory predicated on the deepest truths of the human heart.

Dorothy McGuire, a talented actress who has never received her just due in films, and Robert Young gave excellent performances, as did Herbert Marshall and Mildred Natwick. Ably directed by John Cromwell and produced by the quality-conscious Harriet Parsons (who also produced the 1948 Irene Dunne hit, *I Remember Mama*) the 1945 version had the benefit of a perceptive and literate screenplay by De Witt Bodeen and Herman J. Mankiewicz. Ted Tetzlaff's imaginative photography was not the least of its assets. Roy Webb's music and clever art and set work also helped the total effect.

"The Enchanted Cottage" is all that remains of a great estate on the New England shore. The rest of the building had burned years before in a fire, and this remaining wing has acquired over the years a romantic history, having been used as a honeymoon cottage for young marrieds for as long as they wished. Carved in one of its windowpanes are the names of lovers who came there and found perfect happiness, thanks to the cottage's spell.

As the story opens it is owned by Mildred Natwick, widow of a soldier killed in World War I. She appreciates and understands the strange nature of the house and has as her conscious aim the promotion of love alliances.

She hires as a servant an unattractive, forlorn girl, Miss McGuire, who wants to live there to seek consolation from its atmosphere, which has profoundly moved her. Robert Young, a handsome young flier, comes to rent the cottage for his honeymoon with his beautiful fiancée, Hillary Brooke, but on the eve of his wedding he is called to active duty. Later he is wounded and horribly scarred.

Disconsolate and misanthropic, he comes once again to The Enchanted Cottage, but this time to

Robert Young, Dorothy McGuire and Herbert Marshall

Robert Young and Dorothy McGuire

Dorothy McGuire

hide his face from the world. His relatives and his fiancée arrive to plead with him to return, but he rejects them, and also releases his fiancée from the engagement when he senses her recoil from his scarred face.

Dorothy McGuire and Josephine Whittell

Gradually the mousy, homely domestic and the withdrawn ex-soldier come to know each other, and communication of sorts is established, with the watchful Miss Natwick noting events. Young continues embittered and essentially remote, but Miss McGuire gradually falls in love with him. Then, in an effort to free himself once and for all of his mother's encroachments, he asks her to marry him, making plain his motive: a grotesque "marriage of convenience." Though heartbroken at the realization that he doesn't return her love, Miss McGuire agrees.

But on their honeymoon night in the cottage, a miracle happens. The cottage has wrought its strange spell, and suddenly they are beautiful to each other. Oliver (Young) finds himself handsome again and Laura (Miss McGuire) glows with a newfound loveliness. They try to explain the miracle to their good friend and visitor John Hillgrave (Herbert Marshall), who is blind.

Now rapturously in love, they know for a time a happiness beyond their wildest conceptions. Then his relatives come and thoughtlessly shatter with a few words the illusion they had built up between them, though Hillgrave has tried to warn the intruders in advance.

Suddenly they are ugly again, to themselves as well as to others, back to where they were before the "miracle." But Hillgrave and Abigail (Miss Natwick) in time make them understand that the world cannot destroy their precious illusion as long as their mutual love endures. For the beauty they behold in each other comes, not from the cottage, but from the love they share.

This delicate premise is beautifully realized by the performances of the principals and by their supporting players. Cromwell's direction is probing and precise, mindful always of the fragilities of the tender tale.

The Enchanted Cottage is a story for lovers, for idealists—and yes, for romantics. For in a category of film that in too many instances has proven fustian and contrived, the simple beauty and honest sentiment of this film shine clear and true. Its heart is in the right place, and its basic emotional elements are rooted in the fundamentals of human experience.

Dorothy McGuire and Herbert Marshall

Dorothy McGuire and Robert Young

115

This Love of Ours

Universal

1945

CREDITS: Directed by William Dieterle. Produced by Howard Benedict. Screenplay by Bruce Manning, John Klorer and Leonard Lee, based on the play *As Before, Better than Before* by Luigi Pirandello. Photographed by Lucien Ballard. Music by H. J. Salter. Edited by Frank Gross.

OPENED at Loew's Criterion Theater, New York, October 31, 1945. Running time: 90 minutes.

CAST: Merle Oberon (Karin Tuzac); Charles Korvin (Michel Tuzac); Claude Rains (Targel); Carl Esmond (Uncle Robert); Sue England (Susette); Jess Barker (Chadwick); Harry Davenport (Doctor Wilkerson); Ralph Morgan (Doctor Lane); Fritz Leiber (Doctor Bailey); Helen Thimig (Tucker); Ferike Boros (Housekeeper); Howard Freeman (Doctor Barnes); Selmer Jackson (Doctor Melnik); Dave Willock (Doctor Dailey); Ann Codee (Anne); Andre Charlot (M. Flambertin); Darris Merrick (Vivian); William Edmunds (Jose); Barbara Bates (Mrs. Dailey); Leon Tyler (Ross); Cora Witherspoon (Woman); Maris Wrixon (Evelyn); Robert Raison (Callboy); Evelyn Falke (Nanette); Joanie Bell (Susette as a child).

Merle Oberon and Charles Korvin

Merle Oberon and Charles Korvin

An ironic, psychological play of the famed Italian dramatist, Luigi Pirandello, originally titled *As Before, Better Than Before*, was reworked in 1945 into a highly romantic Universal movie called (leave it to Hollywood!) *This Love of Ours*. Since Pirandello died in 1936, no one will ever know what *he* would have thought of it. Pirandello's plays had been transcribed to movies before (as in Greta Garbo's *As You Desire Me*) and usually dealt with such matters as the difference between appearance and reality and the true, primitive nature of man divorced from the influences of culture and convention.

As transferred to film by screenwriters Bruce Manning, John Klorer and Leonard Lee, Pirandello's abstract ruminations gave way to the love problems of Merle Oberon and Charles Korvin, with director William Dieterle tracing to good effect the labyrinthine agonies of romance gone sour. Lucien Ballard (one of Miss Oberon's offscreen husbands) photographed her flatteringly, and H. J. Salter's

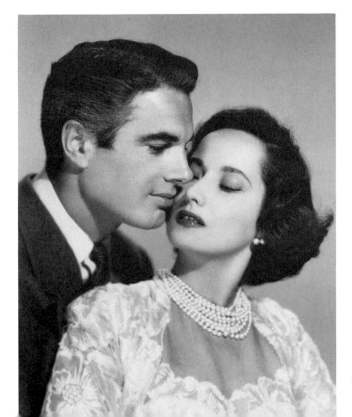

Merle Oberon and Charles Korvin

Charles Korvin and Merle Oberon

music, as is often the case with romantic films, imparted a gorgeous intensity all its own to the hyper-emotional on-screen doings.

The picture was obviously tailored to the express requirements of the exotic and sophisticated Miss Oberon, who suffered throughout the hour-and-a-half running time with a passionate sensibility that was standard, unadulterated Oberon—and in 1945 who could ask for more? As her leading man Universal brought in chiseled-profiled, dulcet-voiced Korvin, and a pictorial pair they made.

The heart appeal is accentuated throughout in a story that opens with a jaded, disillusioned Miss Oberon accompanying philosophical cafe caricaturist Claude Rains in a Chicago bistro. Famed research scientist Korvin, in Chicago for a medical convention, goes out on the town with fellow doctors, Miss Oberon confronts him in the cafe—and attempts suicide. Korvin rushes her to a hospital and saves her life with a complicated operation, but her will to live is obviously not of the strongest.

While guiding her back to recovery he persuades her that their teen-age daughter, Sue England, needs her—yes, *their* daughter—and then it's a flashback to Paris fifteen years before.

It seems that Miss Oberon was a musical comedy star with a traveling show who sprained her ankle onstage and was attended by then-interne Korvin. The troupe went on to a European tour. Oberon stayed on in Paris to romance and marry Korvin. They had a daughter, Susette. All went happily and merrily until neighborhood gossips convinced hard-working doctor Korvin that his pretty young wife was playing around with another man. She was actually innocent, but he hastily condemned her on circumstantial evidence. He then took their little girl and disappeared into the blue, leaving her bereft of all she held dear.

Later he learns his mistake, but by then he cannot find her. He lands a new position in America, raises his daughter—and then comes the Chicago meeting.

Oberon, though still in love with Korvin, cannot forgive him his original distrust and desertion, nor the ten years of loneliness and exile his hasty decision had forced on her, but against friend Rains's advice she goes back with him to his luxurious estate, ostensibly as his "second" wife, because of her child, whom she longs to see again. Oberon's true identity is kept from the girl, who has worshipped her supposedly dead mother's memory with an elaborate garden shrine, and who is a rather moody, misanthropic type who resents the "interloper" and refuses to call her "mother." Rains shows up again in the midst of these domestic complications and plays wise guide and mentor.

The upshot of all this is, of course, predictable. Korvin and Oberon rekindle their original love; after initial rebuffs she begins to make inroads with her child, who still holds aloof—but when a frustrated Oberon decides to leave in despair, the child calls out "Mother!" and all is well, though the girl still hasn't grasped that Oberon is her real mother.

Presumably she will be told at the right time. The broken family is then reunited, and Rains departs giving his paternal—or is it avuncular—blessing.

So much for the story, but it is scrumptiously dressed up by an army of creative artists and technicians to look like the two million dollars it reportedly cost. The scrupulous mounting, evocative, haunting music and overall quality look help things no end, and Miss Oberon and Mr. Korvin make an electric pair. Sue England is brattish and irritating as the daughter who keeps Oberon's maternal instincts frustrated, and Rains is wasted in a part which, his articulate philosophizings aside, condemns him to virtual onlooker status.

Nonetheless the picture has a genuinely romantic look and sound, fits Merle Oberon's mystique like a glove, gives handsome Korvin the Hollywood-gloss treatment, and for all its illogic and windiness, leaves the audience oddly catharsized, a worthy use of two million dollars!

Merle Oberon, Charles Korvin and Joanie Bell

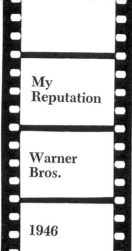

My Reputation

Warner Bros.

1946

CREDITS: Directed by Curtis Bernhardt. Produced by Henry Blanke. Screenplay by Catherine Turney from the novel *Instruct My Sorrows*, by Clare Jaynes. Music by Max Steiner.

OPENED at the Strand Theatre, New York, January 25, 1946. Running time: 94 minutes.

CAST: Barbara Stanwyck (Jessica Drummond); George Brent (Major Scott Landis); Warner Anderson (Frank Everett); Lucile Watson (Mrs. Kimball); John Ridgely (Cary Abbott); Eve Arden (Ginna Abbott); Esther Dale (Anna); Jerome Cowan (George Van Ormand); Leona Maricle (Riette Van Ormand); Scotty Beckett (Kim Drummond); Bobby Cooper (Keith Drummond); Ann Todd (Gretchen Van Ormand); Janis Wilson (Penny Boardman); Darwood Kaye ("Droopy" Hawks).

George Brent and Barbara Stanwyck

Barbara Stanwyck at thirty-seven was at the height of her powers when she filmed *My Reputation* in 1944. It was not released, however, until early 1946, since during that period Warners' implemented a policy of holding up films photographed during 1943–44 (some of which were shown in Army camps) until 1946–47, the idea being to tap the postwar movie attendance boom, which was expected (and correctly) to outmatch the World War II ticket-buying bonanza. Ingrid Bergman's *Saratoga Trunk* and Warners' Olivia de Havilland-Ida Lupino starrer about the Brontës, *Devotion*, also fell into this category, being released at the same time as *My Reputation.*

Made on the heels of one of her biggest hits, *Double Indemnity,* her 1944 *piece de resistance,* Stanwyck's *My Reputation* proved well worth the wait. It was a solid romantic drama about a young widow's readjustment after her husband's terminal illness and death, and it suited the 1946 public mood very well, as many women had gone through similar adjustments during the war.

Director Curtis Bernhardt helped the star to establish the right mood throughout, and Max Steiner's melodic inspirations suited the situations and problems to a "T," as they always did. As her leading man, she drew George Brent, an old hand at helping women suffer through to a denouement sometimes happy, sometimes unhappy, in this case a blend of both. Lucile Watson, Leona Maricle, Eve Arden and John Ridgely lent dependable support, the mounting was first-rate, and the picture proved popular with women moviegoers while suffering initial reviews that were not as fair and objective as they might have been, and which have since been canceled by more charitable and clear-sighted judgments. Possibly the 1946 critics had had their fill of suffering, death, grief, and loneliness, there having been a flood of such pictures during 1944–45, with the tragedies of World War II providing fresh fodder for assorted agonizings—and *My Reputation* caught them at a saturation point.

The film has been revived frequently on television, and has been abominably butchered, with some of Stanwyck's best scenes eliminated. Even so, what remains is powerful and affecting drama.

The picture opens with Stanwyck lying in her darkened bedroom right after her husband's funeral. The mother of two boys, she is pondering the necessary readjustments. Her lawyer tells her in a subsequent scene that if she is careful she can live comfortably on what is left, and can retain the handsome house in the exclusive suburb of Lake Forest, Illinois.

She tries to keep busy with war work, is polite but reserved with friends, resists the overtures of the married wolves of her set who insist that those widows know their onions and are fair game for quick romance. She tries to find comfort in her boys but they have arrived at the early teens and

Barbara Stanwyck

Barbara Stanwyck and George Brent

Barbara Stanwyck and Eve Arden

Bobby Cooper, Lucile Watson, Scotty Beckett, and Barbara Stanwyck

Barbara Stanwyck, Eve Arden, John Ridgely and George Brent

are waxing independent. Determined not to lean on them she sends them off with their young friends, and finally has to see them off to school.

Loneliness and rootlessness dog her constantly, and her emotional and physical hungers rise to smite her. But she is a somewhat prim, conservative, aristocratic type, and her domineering dowager mother, Lucile Watson, introduces added irritations by husband-hunting for her without any excouragement.

She weeps out her woes and tensions to good-old-standby Eve Arden, bright, brittle and compassionate as always, who suggests she take off on a skiing vacation with her and husband John Ridgely. There she meets Brent, a rakish but likable army major on leave, who wants to love her (and presumably leave her), but Stanwyck will have none of it. After twitting her for her hidebound conventionality, Brent leaves her in frustated condition, asking herself the age-old question: *is* virtue its own reward?

Back home in Lake Forest she copes with the honorable suit of stable but dull Warner Anderson, of whom her strait-laced mother approves, but encounters Brent again in a night club and soon she is on the shall-I-or-shall-I-not carousel, debating whether she should snatch quick fulfillment with a man she loves but who has told her he isn't the marrying kind, or settle for the nice, dependable guy.

During the course of resolving such dilemmas, she weathers a barrage of gossip about her allegedly "loose" involvement with the major, her boys turn against her ("Mom, don't you remember dad *at all?*"), she drags the major to a house party thrown by witchy neighbor Leona Maricle, whom she tells off in fine style, winds up trying to explain her loneliness and emotional needs to her sons, gets lectured by her mother ("As you grow older, my dear, you will learn that conventions are there because there is a need for them.") In the middle of all this, Brent informs her he has been transfered to New York and from there overseas, she realizes she will lose her boys if she follows him to the Big Town—and surprise, surprise, he informs her that at last he is himself seriously in love and that when he comes back they will marry.

The fadeout has Stanwyck seeing him off at the railroad station, promising to wait—and then striding off valiantly to Steiner's musical fadeout.

The story plays better—much better—than it reads, because a lot of talented people with a lot to offer have invested it with their best efforts. But *don't* see it on TV; wait for a theatrical revival.

A Stolen Life

Warner Bros.

1946

CREDITS: Directed by Curtis Bernhardt. Produced by Bette Davis as "A B.D. Production." Screenplay by Catherine Turney. Adapted by Margaret Buell Wilder from the novel by Karel J. Benes. Photographed by Sol Polito and Ernest Haller. Art Direction by Robert Haas. Music by Max Steiner. Musical Direction by Leo F. Forbstein. Wardrobe by Orry-Kelly. Edited by Rudi Fehr.

OPENED at the Hollywood Theatre, New York, May 1, 1946. Running time: 109 minutes.

CAST: Bette Davis (Kate Bosworth-Patricia Bosworth); Glenn Ford (Bill Emerson); Dane Clark (Karnak); Walter Brennan (Eben Folger); Charlie Ruggles (Freddie Linley); Bruce Bennett (Jack Talbot); Peggy Knudsen (Deirdre); Esther Dale (Mrs. Johnson); Joan Winfield (Lucy); Clara Blandick (Martha).

Bette Davis's *A Stolen Life* is another picture that was underestimated in its own time and that holds up surprisingly well in its television and theatrical revivals. It was produced by Bette Davis herself for Warners' (the one time she ever doubled as a producer) and it reflects her taste and general philosophy. The reflection is all to the good, for Bette Davis is a true artist, and when she puts her soul into a movie, and moreover dictates its overall conception, as she did in this case, something interestingly valid, esthetically speaking, is bound to emerge.

Obviously, its theme had a strong appeal for her

when she made it in early 1945 (it was not released until spring 1946). At the time she had been a widow for nearly two years, and was going through a lonely, disoriented phase. She married soon after it was completed, and it is interesting to note that the man she wed, William Grant Sherry, was an artist—and artists figured heavily in the picture.

Certainly her acting in *A Stolen Life* reveals a sad, and introspectively searching, Davis that not all her films have caught to such a degree. It is in many respects an introverted picture, with strong emotions coursing beneath the surface, emerging intermittently with a startling force—but always with an artistic validity proper to the mood and situations.

Bette Davis and Glenn Ford

Bette Davis and Dane Clark

Bette Davis and Glenn Ford

She also gave "them" what the publicity flacks called "Double Davis," as in it she played the dual roles of twin sisters, a "good" one and a "bad" one, of course. No doubt this element had added appeal for her, as she was able to offer the two standard Davis on-screen incarnations—the idealistic romantic and the bitchy shrew, both of which she could portray to perfection.

In this "B.D. Production" as the credits termed it, Miss Davis surrounded herself with highly gifted people, and all delivered in fine style, though obviously following her lead and catering to her whims and inspirations.

Curtis Bernhardt, a sensitive, perceptive director who was to guide Miss Davis through other fine pictures like *Payment on Demand*, worked well with her, comprehended her ideas and gave her what she wanted. Catherine Turney wrote a literate and intelligent screenplay, adapted by Margaret Buell Wilder from a story by Karel Benes that Elizabeth Bergner had used for a movie in 1939. (The Davis and Bergner versions are dissimilar in mood and coloration, if not in basic plot.)

For her leading man Miss Davis borrowed Glenn Ford from Columbia, and he proved exactly

Bette Davis and Glenn Ford

right as the shy, sensitive young engineer who repairs to a Martha's Vineyard lighthouse "to get away from too many people." There is a story that director Bernhardt wanted to alter Ford's hesitant speech pattern, one of his attractive trademarks, but Davis said it was just right for the part, and it stayed. (Which offers added evidence that *A Stolen Life*, chosen, produced, acted in, and endlessly-tink-

Charlie Ruggles and Bette Davis

ered-with by dynamo Davis, is about as clear a reflection of her innate nature and outlook on life as anything she has ever done.)

The appealing story has drab, introverted but kind and gentle Pat Bosworth (Davis) venturing to Martha's Vineyard to indulge her painting hobby. She is one of two twin daughters, orphaned, of a wealthy family. Charlie Ruggles is their guardian, Freddie, with whom she stays while on the island. She gets Ford to give her a lift when she misses the boat, sketches him during the two-hour trip, and they form a friendship. She then maneuvers to paint lighthouse-keeper Walter Brennan to be near Ford, and a sensitively conducted romantic relationship develops. Like herself, he is shy, withdrawn, idealistic, deep-spirited, and she hopes they will spend the rest of their lives together, for she has fallen deeply in love.

But in sashays brazen, beautiful Pat, her twin sister, and the other side of Miss Davis's imagistic genie is busily called into action, for Pat swaggers, conducts herself boldly, and pursues every good-looking man within reach. She meets Ford by accident, he thinks she's Kate, the other sister, and tells her she's "different," and like any other man he likes frosting on his cake and he hadn't thought before that she had the frosting. Which encourages vampish Pat to nail him for her own.

Of course the shy Kate takes it very hard when, instead of becoming her husband, the smitten Mr. Ford becomes her brother-in-law instead, and she moons a while until an iconoclastic, proletarian artist, Dane Clark, comes along, and tries to romance her in his crude way ("Woman needs man; man needs woman; that's how it all starts; art, music the works"), but Kate counteracts this by telling him she's sorry but it's "the grand passion for me, or nothing."

Meanwhile her brother-in-law, unconscious of the pain he is inflicting, takes to calling her at times, raising her hopes, but when she realizes he is only being friendly and is just trying to use her to model negligee birthday presents for her sister, her depression deepens even more.

One day she finds herself visiting the Vineyard at the same time as Pat. They take a sailboat ride, and are swept into a storm. Pat drowns while clutching at her with a ringed finger (the ring somehow ends up in Kate's fist) and people think she's her sister. She *lets* them think so because "it seemed my one chance for happiness."

And so, having stolen her sister's life, she finds herself Mrs. Bill Emerson (Ford)—but then come horrid revelations; it seems that Pat was playing around with other men, that Bill knew about it, and was on the point of divorcing her. She asks him for "another chance" and he reluctantly agrees, but when confronted with more evidence of her sister's misdeeds she finds she is not up to the complicated deceptions and flees back to the island.

Ford, sensing at last who she is, follows her there, and high on an Atlantic cliff, swathed in embracing fog, he tells her that it is she he loves, that Pat was only a disillusioning interlude, that he realizes now that they were meant for each other, and that together they must start all over, from the beginning, as if nothing had even been interrupted. All of which constituted one of the more entrancingly cathartic movie fadeouts of 1946 or any year.

The film, especially in the first half, is bathed in a warm, romantic intimacy. Audience empathy is quickly established, and one is rooting for the shy, sensitive Kate to win the man of her dreams, for all his Hamletian indecisiveness. The coincidences are stretched, admittedly; Walter Winchell, in his staccato, decisive way a really perceptive film reporter, said in a 1946 column that the picture was "short on logic but long on heart-appeal," and to a degree he was right. But the sensitivity and creative force of the film so overwhelm the minor flaws of coincidence and forced-situations, that it wins commendation as a romantic mood-piece of fine caliber. Max Steiner aided Davis and Company with a lush romantic score.

A Stolen Life proved extremely popular with the public, which often judges a picture more truly than any reviewers' consensus, and as before noted, it is interesting, among many reasons, for its charming and indeed poignant revelation of Bette Davis's inner processes, psychically and emotionally, during its making.

Bette Davis

Walter Brennan and Bette Davis

127

CREDITS: Directed by Mitchell Leisen. Produced by Charles Brackett. Screenplay by Jacques Thiery and Charles Brackett based on a story by Mr. Brackett. Photographed by Daniel L. Fapp. Special Photographic Effects by Gordon Jennings. Process Photography by Farciot Edouart. Music by Victor Young. Edited by Alma Macrorie.

OPENED at Radio City Music Hall, New York, May 23, 1946. Running time: 122 minutes.

CAST: Olivia de Havilland (Josephine Norris); John Lund (Captain Bart Cosgrove-Gregory Pearson); Mary Anderson (Corinne Pearson); Roland Culver (Lord Desham); Phillip Terry (Alex Pearson); Bill Goodwin (Mac Tilton); Virginia Welles (Liz Lorimer); Victoria Horne (Daisy Gingras); Griff Barnett (Mr. Norris); Alma Macrorie (Belle Ingham); Bill Ward (Gregory as a child); Frank Faylen (Babe); Willard Robertson (Dr. Hunt); Arthur Loft (Mr. Clinton); Virginia Farmer (Mrs. Clinton); Harlan Briggs (Dr. McLaughlin); Doris Lloyd (Mrs. Pringle); Clyde Cook (Mr. Harket); Billy Gray (Billy Igham); Gary Gray (Casey Igham); Chester Clute (Clarence Igham).

Olivia de Havilland and John Lund

Phillip Terry, Bill Goodwin and Olivia de Havilland

*Phillip Terry, Griff Barnett
and Olivia de Havilland*

Olivia de Havilland and producer-scripter Charles Brackett rated a medal for courage in 1946 when they brought out yet another story of the woman who strays off the beaten path and pays for long years afterwards. The basic premise of *To Each His Own*, as of that first of the post-World War II years, was distinctly on the old-fashioned side, yet amazingly (or perhaps not so amazingly) they brought it off.

For one thing, the romantic story was backed up by some realistic ingredients, the acting was first-rate (Miss de Havilland won her first Oscar with it), the direction of Mitchell Leisen extracted all possible values from the intelligently conceived original story by Mr. Brackett, which he and Jacques Thiery hammered into a screenplay, and the whole project, when seen in finished form on the screen, all two hours and two minutes of it, had a solid, substantial look that the story itself would not seem to anticipate, no matter how artful and detailed the production aspects.

Victor Young's music, Daniel Fapp's photography and the sharp editing of Alma Macrorie also played their roles in the happy result.

Olivia de Havilland, left, and John Lund, right

*Phillip Terry, Mary Anderson
and Olivia de Havilland*

The story? Miss Olivia is another of those girls who love too well and not too wisely, and handsome airman John Lund on a war bond tour circa 1918 meets her in Pierson Falls (another of those small Eastern towns where such tragedies usually begin) and—to make a short story shorter—makes her pregnant. Then he gets himself killed in the war. To avoid small-town gossip, druggist's daughter de Havilland has her baby son elsewhere, then tries to reintroduce him back to the hometown by a poorly planned ruse that misfires. Complications abound for the unwed mother when she finds her son firmly ensconced in the home of her rejected suitor, Phillip Terry, and his wife Mary Anderson, who thinks Phillip's the baby's father and takes her revenge on Olivia by holding onto the kid for dear life.

Olivia soon emigrates to New York, where she is determined to become a success and win the money and influence that will get her baby back; she collects scrapbooks and pictures, sent by foster father Terry, rises fast in the world via her well-

*John Lund, Olivia de Havilland,
Phillip Terry and Mary Anderson*

managed cosmetics firm—and soon is in a position to blackmail Miss Anderson into giving her back her son, who is by then five or six years old. It seems that Terry and Anderson are in a financial bind and need de Havilland's approval of a bank loan without which they are wiped out. So the spiteful Miss Anderson has no choice but to return the child.

However, he proves to be so homesick for his "mother and daddy" and so hostile to his real mother that she conceives of it as an act of basic charity to send him back. Her friend and sidekick Bill Goodwin keeps telling her "Let that kid know you're his mother," but she realizes he has been conditioned to the other home and it is too late.

Many years later, in England, she goes to the station to greet her son, now a serviceman in World War II. He still doesn't know she is his mother. He accepts her hospitality halfheartedly while he romances his girlfriend, who is also in service. Then,

through the kindness of an aristocratic friend of de Havilland's, the marriage waiting period is waived and the eager young couple are married in a nightclub with wedding cake, champagne and all, including a tearfully proud Miss de Havilland. She doesn't want the boy to know why she and her friend Roland Culver have gone to all this solicitous bother, but Culver tells her it's high time he knew, gives the son (John Lund in a dual role) some not so subtle hints, and the chastened, solemn-faced young officer goes over and says, "Mother may I have this dance?"

The above may sound pretty sappy when reduced to synopsis, but it plays surprisingly well. The depth and solidity lie in the true performances, the discerning directorial touches, the avoidance of bathos, the toning down of excess sentiment even when it might be forgiven. The writing is literate, the editing is tight, Miss de Havilland *was* the best actress of 1946.

*Bill Goodwin
and Olivia de Havilland*

CREDITS: Directed by Jean Negulesco. Produced by Jerry Wald. Screenplay by Clifford Odets and Zachary Gold. Based on a story by Fannie Hurst. Photographed by Ernest Haller. Art direction by Hugh Reticker. Music conducted by Franz Waxman. Musical Director, Leo F. Forbstein. Music Adviser, Isaac Stern. Miss Crawford's costumes by Adrian. Edited by Rudi Rehr.

OPENED at the Hollywood Theatre, New York, December 25, 1946. Running time, 125 minutes.

CAST: Joan Crawford (Helen Wright); John Garfield (Paul Boray); Oscar Levant (Sid Jeffers); J. Carroll Naish (Rudy Boray); Joan Chandler (Gina); Tom D'Andrea (Phil Boray); Peggy Knudsen (Florence); Ruth Nelson (Esther Boray); Craig Stevens (Monte Loeffler); Paul Cavanaugh (Victor Wright); Richard Gaines (Bauer); John Abbott (Rozner); Bobby Blake (Paul as a child); Tommy Cook (Phil as a child); Don McGuire (Eddie); Fritz Leiber (Hagerstrom); Peg La Centra (Nightclub Singer); Richard Walsh (Teddy).

John Garfield and Joan Crawford

Joan Crawford had gone to Warner Brothers in 1943 after a disappointing and frustrating final period at Metro-Goldwyn-Mayer, where her pictures had declined in quality despite her efforts to obtain better stories. It took her two years to find *Mildred Pierce*, and it won her an Oscar and immediately transformed her into Bette Davis's most formidable rival at the Burbank studio.

Humoresque, which she was making in early 1946 at the time she received her Academy Award, was the second of her "Big Three" Warner films of the mid-1940's, the first being *Mildred Pierce* and the third *Possessed* (1947). All were so well done that Louis B. Mayer, who regretted his earlier professional parting with Miss Crawford (though they always remained good personal friends) reportedly screened the three for his executives and later asked them, "Why aren't we making pictures like this now at MGM?"

Humoresque contains Crawford's finest performance out of her eighty-odd pictures. I am inclined to suspect that the chief reason for her excellence in it was the heightened confidence in her powers she had gained from that long-sought, long-denied, finally attained Oscar, and she approached the complex role of Helen Wright with sharpened perceptions and an emotional exhilaration that she had seldom accorded to the inferior vehicles she was all too often handed.

The Fannie Hurst story about a New York violinist's rise to fame had been made as a silent in 1920. John Garfield was set for the male lead and the story was originally built around him. Miss Crawford felt that the relatively small role of Helen Wright offered strong possibilities as something in which she could shine, and that it would prove a worthy follow-up to *Mildred Pierce*, and in this her instinct was right. First, however, it became necessary to redo the screenplay, building up her part to make it at least equal to Garfield's. When she won the Oscar in the middle of shooting, the mounting production values were improved, more money put into the picture, and she wound up getting top billing and taking the movie away from Garfield, as her authoritative star-glamour proved irresistible to audiences.

Certainly much money and care were poured into the expanded and embellished *Humoresque*, and over the years it has survived the initial mediocre reviews and proved its enduring worth, as does many another picture insufficiently appreciated in its own time.

The film eventually ran to 125 minutes, and was one of Warners' top 1946 specials, debuting in New York on Christmas Day. Jean Negulesco directed with care, Clifford Odets and Zachary Gold wrote a literate screenplay, producer Jerry Wald poured on the supportive gloss and Bette Davis's favorite cameraman, Ernie Haller, was told to make Crawford look out-of-this-world, which he proceeded to do. (Never has she been more glamorously and strikingly photographed!)

Franz Waxman conducted the ambitious musi-

Joan Crawford

John Garfield

Joan Crawford and John Garfield

cal score with musical direction by Leo Forbstein, and Isaac Stern served as musical adviser. Symphonic scores by such composers as Bizet, Rossini and Wagner proliferated on the sound track. They even threw in a colorfully fussbudgeting Oscar Levant as Garfield's pianist sidekick.

The story has Garfield, a boy from the slums, "adopted" by wealthy and dissolute socialite Crawford, who happens to be saddled with a cynically indulgent husband (Paul Cavanaugh) whose presence she barely acknowledges. When she hears Garfield play at one of her soirees, she's hooked, and the self-appointed patroness introduces him to top impresarios, finances his initial concert, and starts romancing him. But her nature—jaded, neurotic, complex, sybaritic—has made her a failure at love, though presumably a wow at sex (in Production-Code-dominated 1946 they didn't go into *that* aspect) and when she realizes finally that there is no future

happiness for her and Garfield, she decides she has had enough of life and its aridities and bewilderments and walks into the ocean from her beach house, to the accompaniment of the Wagner "Liebestod" which Garfield is playing over the radio from a concert hall.

Prior to this melodramatic but effective denouement, she has been given wryly cynical advice by her forbearing husband, has been told by Garfield's mother that they are wrong for each other and should part, and has gone through jealous moments over a younger woman she thinks Garfield is interested in. She also drinks more than is good for her, surrounds herself with a coterie of lacquered studs, and is given to overly sardonic aphorisms and self-deprecations. It's all too overwhelming, "the world is too much with her," and she realizes that she will only pull Garfield down and not help herself. Hence the ocean, and presumably peace.

Oscar Levant and John Garfield

John Garfield and Ruth Nelson

The movie is filled with romantically lush scenes: Crawford in a concert box responding with glistening eyes and slightly parted lips to Garfield's intense violin playing, Crawford in a dim bar reproaching Garfield irrationally and ordering fresh drinks at five-minute intervals, Crawford, with a sort of iron-butterfly wistfulness, asking Garfield's coldly disapproving mother how old he was in the kid picture holding the violin, Crawford, surrounded by her tuxedoed studs, ridiculing *enfant terrible* Garfield as he plays at her house party (yes he puts her down)—and last, but not least certainly, Crawford staggering along the ocean sands to oblivion as the shining tides under the moonlight edge toward the hem of her gown and the last strains of Wagner die way from the distant radio.

A romantic picture? Rather. And all concerned do full justice to it—even Garfield, who considering his evident disadvantages in the face of that hurricane of glamour, managed to weather it pretty well.

John Garfield and Ruth Nelson

135

Song
of
Love

Metro-
Goldwyn-
Mayer

1947

CREDITS: Produced and directed by Clarence Brown. Screenplay by Robert Ardrey, Allen Vincent, Irmgard Von Cube, Ivan Tors. Based on the play by Bernard Schubert and Mario Silva. Photographed by Harry Stradling. Art Direction by Cedric Gibbons. Edited by Robert J. Kern. Set Decorations by Edwin B. Willis. Musical Direction by Bronislau Kaper. Sound Recording by Douglas Shearer. Piano recordings by Arthur Rubinstein. William Steinberg conducting the MGM Symphony Orchestra. Costumes supervised by Irene, with women's costumes by Walter Plunkett. St. Luke's Boy Choir. Musical Adviser, Laura Dubman.

CAST: Katharine Hepburn (Clara Wieck Schumann); Paul Henreid (Robert Schumann); Robert Walker (Johannes Brahms); Henry Daniell (Franz Liszt); Leo G. Carroll (Professor Wieck); Else Janssen (Bertha); Gigi Perreau (Julie); "Tinker" Furlong (Felix); Ann Carter (Marie); Janine Perreau (Eugenie); Jimmie Hunt (Ludwig); Anthony Sydes (Ferdinand); Eilene Janssen (Elsie); Roman Bohnen (Dr. Hoffman); Ludwig Stossel (Haslinger); Tala Birell (Princess Valerie Hohenfels); Kurt Katch (Judge); Henry Stephenson (King Albert); Konstantin Shayne (Reinecke); Josephine Whittell (Lady In Box); Byron Foulger (Court Officer).

*Paul Henreid
and Katharine Hepburn*

One of the high spots of Katharine Hepburn's MGM years (1940–1952) was the 1947 production, *Song of Love*. In it she played Clara Schumann, pianist wife of composer Robert Schumann and mother of his seven children. Robert Walker was also on hand as the young Johannes Brahms, also destined for immortal musical fame, who comes to live with Clara and Robert, falls in love with Clara, and then departs sorrowfully when she rejects his love. The basic story deals with the domestic life of the Schumanns, their early struggles against poverty, Robert's disappointments in his career, the gradual emergence of a fame that came only slowly and painfully for him; the ominous ringings in his ears that presaged his insanity and early death, and Clara's efforts as a widow to publicize her husband's unique talent with extensive concert tours.

Historical purists, to say nothing of music buffs, may quibble with the myriad bowdlerizations of the actualities of Schumann domestic and career affairs, also the gratuitously one-sided infatuation of Brahms for Clara. But the glamour mills of Hollywood have by long tradition demanded in advance a suspension of disbelief, or at least they have implied such a demand, and the romantic settings and ambience, the fine music expertly performed, the lush accoutrements of this expensive picture tended to mute (or possibly overwhelm) the quibblers, such as they were.

Miss Hepburn had perhaps the most glamorous, full-bodied role of her three-Oscar-winning career, and was ably directed by Clarence Brown, who also produced. She ran the gamut from the dewy-eyed bride who defies her family to marry Schumann to

Katharine Hepburn and Paul Henrei

Katharine Hepburn and Paul Henreid

Leo G. Carroll, Katharine Hepburn, Paul Henreid

Katharine Hepburn, Gigi Perreau and Roman Bohnen

the earnest, conscientious, loving mother, to the talented pianist who appears to public acclaim, to the tortured wife of a man slowly going mad to the widow who determines to perpetuate the memory of the man she loved.

There are many telling scenes: the New Year's party where a game of fortunes is played and Robert's "prize" turns out to be a coffin, the efforts of Liszt to promote Robert's music for snobbish audiences spurned by Clara in a subtle put-down scene where she replays the Schumann music Liszt had performed too grandiloquently, pointing out to the overly confident but well-meaning Franz that her husband's music must be rendered simply and sincerely; her shocked concern when her husband's affliction overtakes him while conducting an orchestra; her poignant sorrow when her husband, now incarcerated in an asylum, blithely informs her he has written a new work and proceeds to play something he had composed long years before.

Henry Daniell is fine as Franz Liszt, who tried sincerely to publicize Schumann's music to the world but encountered difficulties in winning wide acceptance for his friend from obtuse German music-lovers. Walker is somewhat callow as the young Johannes Brahms, and his self-sacrifice for the Schumanns seems forced and contrived. *Song of Love* is actually Miss Hepburn's picture all the way, though Henreid is often persuasive as the talented but hapless Schumann, whose strange music often reproduces the mania that stalks him. Miss Hepburn covers the whole spectrum of emotions in a convincing manner, and displays a versatility, combined with a welcome diminution of her usual distracting mannerisms, that does full justice to the Hollywood (if not the actual) image of Clara Schumann.

The lush romanticism is not stinted, and all departments reinforce its omnipresence. Artur Rubinstein played the piano for Hepburn, and she was thoroughly coached by a Rubinstein associate, Laura Dubman, in the correct fingering and other pianistic skills required for filmic verisimilitude. The MGM Symphony Orchestra got across all the passion and force of nineteenth-century music when the Romantic Movement flourished in Europe as never before or since.

The scenario by Ivan Tors, Irmgard Von Cube, Allen Vincent and Robert Ardrey took admitted liberties with the actual lives of its subjects, though not to the blatant extent the screenwriers of *A Song To Remember* had done two years previously.

The overall result was a handsome, often affecting, and grandiosely conceived drama against a rich musical and historical setting—a welcome vacation (for her fans if not for Hepburn) from the Tracy films, and an added demonstration to her admirers—and at a time when it was needed—that Katharine Hepburn, when she put her mind to it, could be a romantic star who took second place to none.

Robert Walker, Katharine Hepburn and Paul Henreid (right)

Paul Henreid, Ludwig Stossel and Katharine Hepburn

Letter From An Unknown Woman

Universal-International

1948

CREDITS: Directed by Max Ophuls. A Ramparts Production. Produced by John Houseman. Screenplay by Howard Koch, from the story by Stefan Zweig. Photographed by Frank Planer. Music by Daniele Amfitheatrof, orchestrated by David Tomkin. Art Direction by Alexander Golitzen. Edited by Ted J. Kent.

OPENED at the Rivoli Theatre, New York, April 28, 1948. Running time: 86 minutes.

CAST: Joan Fontaine (Lisa Berndl); Louis Jourdan (Stefan Brand); Mady Christians (Frau Berndl); Marcel Journet (Johann Stauffer); Art Smith (John); Carol Yorke (Marie); Howard Freeman (Herr Kastner); John Good (Lieutenant Leopold Von Koltnegger); Leo B. Pessin (Stefan Jr.); Erskine Sanford (Porter); Otto Waldis (Concierge); Sonja Bryden (Frau Spitzer).

Unrequited love is the bitterest of all sorrows, as poets have been reminding us for centuries. As Walt Whitman wrote: "Sometimes with one I love, I fill myself with rage for fear I effuse unreturn'd love. But now I know there is no unreturn'd love; the pay is certain one way or another. I loved a certain person ardently and my love was not return'd. Yet out of that I have written these songs . . ."

The theme of unrequited love has recurred frequently in films. One of the most creative examples was the 1948 release, *Letter From An Unknown Woman*. In a 1966 article, "Great Romantic Films Of The Past," I called it "a masterpiece of lyric moods, handsome photography, and sensitive dramatic shadings." Max Ophuls, a European director of uncommon artistry, showcased for compelling results the delicate sensibilities of Joan Fontaine, resulting in her most effective performance (*Rebecca*, *The Constant Nymph* and her Academy Award-winning *Suspicion* notwithstanding).

In 1947 Miss Fontaine indulged in a joint producing venture with her then-husband, William Dozier, which they called Rampart Productions, releasing through Universal-International. She herself initiated the screen version of this haunting story by Stefan Zweig. At the time Miss Fontaine said she wanted a story that would appeal to women, and to her credit she was one of the first to infer that a well conceived and executed woman's picture could attain the depth and universality of true art, a point that far too many denigrators of "women's fare" have missed. For if a picture (a well-done one, that is) appeals to half the human race, it is shortsighted to castigate it as "high-grade soap opera" or "strictly for the ladies" or "matinee handkerchief fodder." Since women have had their fair and full share in the initiation of much art over the centuries, inspiring painting, sculpture, poetry, plays and films, it is esthetically myopic to maintain that pictures which appeal to women primarily are, per se, devoid of artistic validity.

Certainly *Letter From An Unknown Woman* was a consummate work of art, misunderstood by some 1948 critics who labeled it mere sentimental nostalgia or worse. The built-in irony is that *men* were the prime creators of this film in its production, direction and writing phases, as indeed they were in so many other films of the romantic school. A greater realization of this should help put the "woman's picture" cliche to rest for all time, for if a host of creative males can comprehend the feminine psyche so well as to depict its manifestations effectively on screen, the essential universality of feminine emotions becomes obvious. Despite the now-fast-receding fashion of male surface impassivity and stoicism, it grows ever more apparent (certainly since 1948) that romance, tenderness, sentiment, unrequited love, nostalgic yearning, mystical intuition, etc. are as indigenous to the male as to the female, all men being born of women—a point the Europeans appreciated long before the more self-conscious Americans.

Leo B. Pessin and Joan Fontaine

Joan Fontaine

Louis Jourdan, Joan Fontaine and Marcel Journet

141

Joan Fontaine

Seldom has the "unrequited love" theme been given as serious and thorough a going-over as in this picture. John Houseman produced, the screenplay was by Howard Koch, Frank Planer handled the camera work, Daniele Amfitheatrof composed the music (which featured exquisitely inventive variations on the film's essential *leitmotif*, Franz Liszt's piano work, "II Sospiro" ("The Sigh"). Alexander Golitzen did the art work and Ted Kent edited— men all, a point that cannot be stressed too often.

Carol Yorke and Joan Fontaine

Surrounded by the variegated efforts of these creative males, Joan Fontaine, then thirty and at the height of her delicate blonde loveliness (she was one of the most beautiful women ever to grace the screen), gave the most exquisite performance of her career, running the gamut from age fourteen to age twenty-nine as the idealistic girl who falls in love with a handsome young concert pianist (Louis Jourdan) who lives in a neighboring flat in a Vienna apartment house, circa 1885. Enamored from her first sight of him, she listens dreamily to his playing from the garden below and wistfully watches his numerous shallow affairs.

When her mother (Mady Christians) remarries and they move to another city, she continues to yearn for the pianist, whom alone of all men she loves. Years later, now a lovely young woman, she rejects the marriage proposal of a handsome young Army officer (John Good) to return to Vienna and seek out Jourdan.

A model in a dress shop, she stands across the street from his flat night after night. Attracted by her beauty and availability, the pianist picks her up, wines and dines her, then makes love to her for one night; after which, in born-philanderer fashion, he goes off on a concert tour and proceeds to forget all about her. She bears his son in secret. ("I wanted to be the one woman who asked him for nothing.") Later she weds a middle-aged Austrian aristocrat (Marcel Journet) who offers protection and affection as well as a name for young Stefan. But her heart remains starved for the reciprocal ecstasies and fulfillments of true love, and one night, at the opera, she sees her love again. Fifteen years have now passed since first she loved him; seven since she conceived his child.

Now, in 1900, he is an aging roué who had sacrificed art to hedonism. Jaded, lonely in his floundering, rootless existence, Jourdan expresses what she conceives to be a need for her, and she leaves her heartbroken and angered husband to return to him, but then comes fresh disillusion. To her aging but still attractive musician she is only just another fresh conquest. "I came to offer you my whole life— and you didn't even remember me," she ruminates as she leaves his apartment.

Fontaine and her small son have meanwhile contracted typhus in an infected railway carriage. After the boy dies she writes Jourdan a long letter from the hospital telling him in detail of the course of her love for him from the very beginning, and of the fifteen years of suffering and hopeless longing she experienced because of him. She encloses pictures of young Stefan, who was named for him, and among her final words is the phrase: "I love you now as I have always loved you . . ." After which her pen fails and she dies. The letter is sent to Jourdan by one of the nursing nuns at the hospital, who adds the postscript, "May God have mercy on you both."

Meanwhile the grief-stricken husband has challenged Jourdan to a duel, and the cynical ladies' man is about to flee Vienna until the affair, which he shrugs off as just another of his dalliances, cools off. But upon reading the lettter, which arrives via messenger in the middle of the night, he is so deeply moved that he goes out to fight the duel after all. He pins on his lapel one of the blossoms Fontaine had brought him at their final meeting, and in one of the most touching final scenes in film history, Jourdan looks back from the gate to the door, trying to remember the girl who had loved him for fifteen years—and then again he sees her, a wraith of fourteen shyly holding the door open for him as she had done long ago. He smiles at the vision and then enters the coach that will take him to the duel with her husband, and possibly to his own doom.

Letter From An Unknown Woman is replete with sensitively conceived, mystically haunting scenes. Fontaine at fourteen, cringing miserably on the landing as the young man she loves sneaks a woman-of-the-evening into his flat in the dead of a Vienna night, her return from the railroad station on the night her mother moves, for one final glimpse or sound of her beloved, her patient stance outside in the snow, when, as a beautiful young woman, she hopes to catch his eye, the white flowers she buys for him when, after having left her husband, she goes to offer herself to the one man she has ever loved, one final time.

The authenticity and exactness of the Hollywood sets depicting street scenes and interiors of Old Vienna is a tribute to Alexander Golitzen's taste and selectivity. Frank Planer's photography is a creative blend of inventive placement and subtle arrangement of light and shade. Ophuls's direction was never more sharp and sensitive, with gemlike shadings in performances reflecting his attentive guidance, and the low-key but eloquent acting styles blended, modulated and honed to perfection. (In fact, the composite creativity of these men, as displayed in this superior film, call readily to mind the psychologist who wrote that the fear of American boys and men that they will be labeled "sissies" if they reject the "supermasculine" ethic in favor of the indulgence of whatever creative bents they possess, is the factor chiefly responsible for the scandalous loss of male esthetic talent in this country.)

Letter From An Unknown Woman contains not only Miss Fontaine's finest performance, but Jourdan's. With piercing psychological cunning (and aided, no doubt, by Ophuls's creative instincts) Jourdan depicts the self-centered, self-contained, sensually self-indulgent nature of a certain type of artist; tellingly he illustrates (as does Miss Fontaine) the truth of George Santayana's famous phrase (from his 1936 novel, *The Last Puritan*, a poignant study of still another form of unrequited love): "The inspiration of a profound desire, fixed upon some lovely image, is what is called love."

Joan Fontaine

Joan Fontaine and Marcel Journet

Max Ophuls, right, instructing Joan Fontaine on scene

Enchantment

Samuel Goldwyn-RKO

1948

CREDITS: Directed by Irving Reis. Produced by Samuel Goldwyn. Screenplay by John Patrick from the novel *Take Three Tenses* by Rumer Godden. Music by Hugo Friedhofer. Musical direction by Emil Newman. Photographed by Gregg Toland. Song by Dan Raye and Gene De Paul. Edited by Daniel Mandell.

OPENED at the Astor Theatre, New York, December 26, 1948. Running time: 102 minutes.

CAST: David Niven (General Sir Roland Dane); Teresa Wright (Lark Ingoldsby); Evelyn Keyes (Grizel Dane); Farley Granger (Pilot Pax Masterson); Jayne Meadows (Selina Dane); Leo G. Carroll (Proutie); Philip Friend (Pelham Dane); Shepperd Strudwick (Marchese del Laudi); Henry Stephenson (General Fitzgerald); Colin Keith-Johnston (The Eye); Gigi Perreau (Lark as a child); Peter Miles (Rollo as a child); Sherlee Collier (Selina as a child); Warwick Gregson (Pelham as a child); Marjorie Rhodes (Mrs. Sampson); Edmond Breon (Uncle Bunny); Gerald Olivier Smith (Willoughby); Melville Cooper (Jeweler); Dennis McCarthy (Lance Corporal); Gaylord Pendleton (RAF officer); Matthew Boulton (Air Raid Warden); Robin Hughes (Corporal); William Johnstone (Narrator).

Philip Friend dancing with Teresa Wright

Farley Granger and Evelyn Keyes

Enchantment, like *The House on 56th Street* and *The Enchanted Cottage*, is the romance of a house, but this time it's a London domicile, 99 Wiltshire Place to be exact, and the time span is some fifty years (roughly 1894 to 1944).

And what transpires in this particular house? Well, it seems that in the dim past an orphan named Lark Ingoldsby had come there as the old master's ward. When he died she grew up surrounded by the love of the two sons (David Niven and Philip Friend) and the jealous hatred of the daughter, her foster-sister (Jayne Meadows) who humiliates Lark at every turn and wants nothing so much as to marry her off to the first eligible swain to be rid of her for good.

But Lark (Teresa Wright) is a spirited lass with a mind of her own, and she is in love with Rollo (Niven) who loves her but is not sure (at least not yet) if he is *in* love with her, or perhaps he never thinks of it. Meanwhile pretty Lark bides her time, warding off Selina's assorted meannesses, rejecting the suit of Rollo's brother Pelham (Philip Friend) who is also smitten with her, and tolerating the romantic attentions of the Marchese del Laudi (Shepperd Strudwick) who proposes to marry her and carry her off to Italy, never to be seen again (or so Selina hopes).

Rollo is slow to realize that he reciprocates Lark's passion, as before noted, but the sight of her in a fetching ball gown and the intimate coziness of a library fire bring him to his senses and he and Lark announce their impending alliance to Selina. But she will have none of it. The idea of headstrong Lark as her sister-in-law possesses scant appeal, and she maneuvers an appointment to the Indian Command for Rollo via a contact, General Fitzgerald (Henry Stephenson).

Rollo is informed that he must serve for some years, and that Lark must wait for him patiently during those years, as officers apparently cannot take their wives to India with them. He hesitates briefly but just long enough for Lark to throw up her hands in despair (especially after a nasty scene with Selina) and go off to Italy with the Marchese. Rollo, enraged with Selina for interfering with his love for Lark, informs her that he will never again set foot in the house as long as she lives, and throws the key on the floor.

Fifty years later, an ancient retired general, he comes back from India to the now-empty house, filled with memories that both torment and console him. The point is made that love is a magnetic force which exists like an electric charge and pervades certain places where it had once held forth. Here the old officer now takes up his abode, accompanied only by the equally ancient butler Proutie (Leo G. Carroll) who remembers when.

Crusty, grouchy and reclusive, the old man lives within himself, and the house, while elegant in its appointments, is grim in its ambience. It is now the period of World War II and along comes ambulance driver Grizel Dane (Evelyn Keyes), his grand-

David Niven and Jayne Meadows

Philip Friend dancing (center) with Teresa Wright

niece from America, and she gradually wins the
love and acceptance of old Rollo after a grumpy
initial encounter. Pax Masterson (Farley Granger)
a Canadian flier and the nephew of Lark, also puts
in an appearance. The predictable occurs, and the
romantic ambience of the house gets to the kids,
too, and they fall in love.

But Grizel is a cold, practical sort, cautious because she was once hurt by love, and she wants to

David Niven and Evelyn Keyes

wait for Pax till after the war. She sends the disappointed boy away but the old general counsels
her *not* to wait because Love is a precious and fragile thing, and a door may close, a hesitation may
forego, and all is lost forever. So Grizel goes seeking
Pax during an air raid and a bomb hits the house.
The old general joins Lark in death (she had died
in Italy a short time before).

That, then, is *Enchantment*, and it is dressed up
with the expert photography of Gregg Toland (his
last assignment before his death), sensitively directed by Irving Reis, and well written by John
Patrick, who adapted it from the Rumer Godden
novel, *Take Three Tenses*.

Hugo Friedhofer's music, directed by Emil Newman, is charmingly evocative, the settings are handsome and authentic-looking, the acting by all hands
is exactly what it should be for a piece of this
sort—and the overall quality of a Samuel Goldwyn
picture is everywhere in evidence.

The message of *Enchantment* is simple but it is
a romantic one assuredly: Love must be seized for
the moment passes; the spirit of a house can affect
the transmigration of love from soul to soul.

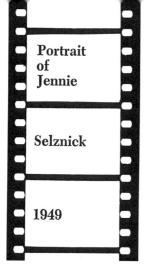

Portrait of Jennie

Selznick

1949

CREDITS: Directed by William Dieterle. SRO (Selznick Releasing Organization) release of a David O. Selznick Production. Screenplay by Paul Osborn and Peter Berneis, based on the novel by Robert Nathan. Adaptation by Leonard Bercovici. Photographed (with Technicolor sequence) by Joseph August. Music by Dimitri Tiomkin, based on variations on Debussy themes. "Jennie's Song" by Bernard Herrmann. Special effects by Clarence Seifer. Process and miniature photography by Paul Eagler. Edited by Gerald Wilson.

OPENED at the Rivoli Theatre, New York, March 29, 1949. Running time: 86 minutes.

CAST: Jennifer Jones (Jennie Appleton); Joseph Cotten (Eben Adams); Ethel Barrymore (Miss Spinney); Cecil Kellaway (Mrs. Matthews); Florence Bates (Mrs. Jekes, The Landlady); Esther Somers (Mrs. Bunce, Her Friend); David Wayne (Gus O'Toole); Albert Sharpe (Mr. Moore); John Farrell (The Policeman); Felix Bressart (The Old Doorman); Maude Simmons (Clara Morgan); Lillian Gish (Mother Mary of Mercy); Clem Bevans (Captain Caleb Cobb); Robert Dudley (An Old Mariner); Henry Hull (Eke).

Joseph Cotten and Jennifer Jones

"An ageless love can cross frontiers of time and death, and neither time nor space need be a barrier to those who refuse to find them so. . . ." This expresses the essential philosophy of the David O. Selznick production, *Portrait of Jennie*, an affecting study of a supernatural romance that showcased Jennifer Jones at her most ethereal and gave Joseph Cotten one of his more winning characterizations.

William Dieterle directed this tasteful film, shot in 1947 on location in New York and New England, and released in early 1949. Based on the delicate mood-piece novella *Portrait of Jennie*, by Robert Nathan, published in 1940, it deals with a young New York painter (Cotten), down on his luck in the Depression year 1932, who despairs because his work lacks depth and pictorial allusiveness. He is

Joseph Cotten and Jennifer Jones

encouraged by a motherly art dealer, Ethel Barrymore, who buys his watercolors and urges him to find new avenues of expression.

One day he meets Jennie Appleton (Miss Jones), a little girl dressed in old-fashioned clothing, in Central Park. He finds the encounter a strangely haunting one, and it is repeated over the months from winter through spring into summer, with the little girl maturing into an adolescent and then into a young woman on the verge of college graduation.

Jennie is strange, speaks of things long past, her speech and manner redolent of another era. Yet she and Eben, the painter, establish a spiritual intimacy, and soon he is in love with her.

He persuades her on one of her unexpected visits to pose for a portrait, and when he finishes it and shows it to Miss Barrymore and her associate, Cecil Kellaway, they are surprised and deeply impressed by its haunting loveliness and spiritual profundity. Meanwhile Jennie, who on her first appear-

148

ance as a little girl, had sung for him a strange song with its only words: "Where I came from, nobody knows, where I am going everyone goes," seems restless and concerned, and portents indicate that they will soon be parted forever.

Through information she has given him at random, he traces her back through time, visiting people who had acquaintance with "Jennie Appleton"—an old vaudeville-house attendant who had kept scrapbooks of her parents, killed in a high-wire act, and a photo of Jennie, looking much as Eben had seen her. The trail leads eventually to the nun at Jennie's college (Lillian Gish), who tells him that Jennie had died in a great hurricane up in New England in the 1920s.

Eben refuses to believe that Jennie is lost to him, and follows his instinct up to Cape Cod, where he finds himself caught in an offshore storm identical with that which had taken Jennie's life. She appears to him during the hurricane, tells him they will never be spiritually parted, and then disappears into the spray, though he tries desperately to hold on to her.

He believes her words, and when he finds her scarf, he feels he has concrete proof that they are, indeed, forever united in spirit and that they will be together in eternity when his own time comes.

Such a theme is, of course, fragile and delicate in the extreme, and when the film was released in 1949, it was unfavorably compared by some critics with the Nathan novel, a few offering the opinion that the theme read better than it filmed.

I have always thought it a moving and beautiful film, its thesis valid in spirit if not provable by human logic. Paul Osborn and Peter Berneis made every effort to forge a screenplay that faithfully reflected the spirit of the original, and to my mind they largely succeeded.

The photography is particularly fine, and Joseph August's color sequences, interspersed with the prevailing black-and-white, are most effective. Clarence Seifer's special effects are commendable, and the process and miniature photography of Paul Eagler is inventive.

The famed hurricane sequence at the end, which was seen on a super-cycloramic screen in some houses especially equipped for it, was a masterpiece of photographic technology and was widely hailed for its inventiveness. The music is an added asset, with Dimitri Tiomkin weaving throughout the film some enchanting variations on Claude Debussy's loveliest themes, most notably *The Afternoon of a Faun*.

The performances are first-rate, with Jennifer Jones catching the elusive nuances of a girl who is spirit rather than flesh; her portrayal of Jennie Appleton, the girl who transcended barriers of time, dissolution, place and spirit to reach out to her true love, is one of her finest, and Joseph Cotten is sensitive and highly responsive to the unusual theme and treatment, giving the delicate story a substance

Joseph Cotten

and reality that at times it needs. Ethel Barrymore, Kellaway, Miss Gish, Florence Bates and David Wayne all lend sterling support.

Of *Portrait of Jennie* it can be said, as the Catholic devout say of alleged miracles: "For those with faith, no explanation is necessary; for those without it, no explanation is possible."

Those who feel that Death represents but a temporary parting of loving spirits will draw comfort from this film today as in 1949, and those who see in Death mere annihilation and oblivion will, at the very least, be accorded food for thought. And those who believe in Love as a universal, timeless, all-encompassing force will find *Portrait of Jennie* one of its more compelling and touching expressions.

CREDITS: Directed by William Wyler. A William Wyler Production. Screenplay by Ruth and Augustus Goetz from their stage play, suggested by Henry James's *Washington Square*. Photographed by Leo Tover. Music by Aaron Copland. Art Direction by John Meehan. Set Decorations by Emile Kurt. Song "My Love Loves Me" by Ray Evans and Jay Livingston. Some Copland themes woven around Eighteenth Century air, "Plaisir d'Amour." Set Designer, Henry Horner. Edited by William Hornbeck.

OPENED at Radio City Music Hall, October 6, 1949. Running time: 115 minutes.

CAST: Olivia de Havilland (Catherine Sloper); Montgomery Clift (Morris Townsend); Ralph Richardson (Doctor Austin Sloper); Miriam Hopkins (Lavinia Penniman); Vanessa Brown (Maria); Mona Freeman (Marion Almond); Betty Linley (Mrs. Montgomery); Selena Royle (Elizabeth Montgomery); Paul Lees (Arthur Townsend); Harry Townsend (Mr. Abeel); Russ Conway (Quintus); David Thursby (Geier).

Miriam Hopkins, Montgomery Clift, Ralph Richardson and Olivia de Havilland

Olivia de Havilland won her second Academy Award for *The Heiress*, and it was well deserved, for this hardworking, sincere actress gave one of her most thoughtful performances in this screen version of the Ruth and Augustus Goetz play, with screenplay also by the Goetzes, based on Henry James's *Washington Square*.

The picture also contains what I consider to be Sir Ralph Richardson's finest all-time performance as Dr. Austin Sloper, the tyrannical patriarch of 16 Washington Square circa 1850, who gives his daughter condescension but not love, and deplores her lack of resemblance to her charming, beautiful and accomplished mother, who died in youth. Montgomery Clift, too, gives one of his better performances as the fortune-hunting Morris Townsend.

Credit for these performances, as well as for a superior picture, is due in no small measure to di-

Montgomery Clift and Olivia de Havilland

Ralph Richardson, Olivia de Havilland, Montgomery Clift, Miriam Hopkins

Ralph Richardson, Montgomery Clift and Olivia de Havilland

rector William Wyler, whose peculiar gift (among many) was the ability to elicit from actors special qualities and insights that they themselves did not realize they had: he did this for Bette Davis in *Jezebel*, for Laurence Olivier in *Wuthering Heights*, for Miriam Hopkins in *These Three*, among many others, and his infinite capacity for taking pains, a hallmark of genius, is again apparent in the performances of the three principals of *The Heiress*.

Wyler, of course, had the benefit of a superior script, polished, literate, perceptive; faithful to the speech and manners of its era; and the photography of Leo Tover, the art work of John Meehan and the distinctive, evocative music of Aaron Copland recaptured the Washington Square ambience of the mid-nineteenth century with a sure artistry founded on endless research and careful conceptualizing—all of which make *The Heiress* a cinematic gem.

Like all true cinematic art, *The Heiress* reflects the original artist, in this case the consummate psychologist Henry James. It is a handsomely romantic film—romantic in its settings, its costumes, its music, its overall flavor and atmosphere. It is a delightful blend of the intelligent, the escapist and the realistic, the tender and the dry—elements that can be made to coalesce only if blended by masters. Mastery is apparent in every aspect of this production.

The story has a universal appeal. It tells of Catherine Sloper (de Havilland), a shy, plain girl of the greatest good will who wants only to please the father she loves, yet seems to elicit only his testy disapproval in matters great and small. She is an heiress—she has $10,000 a year from her late mother and will receive another $20,000 on her father's death ($30,000 a year was considered immensely rich in 1850) and by all the rules should have been courted by a parade of young aristocrats reaching around the block. However, her gawky stance, her plain demeanor, her lack of charm, put them off.

But along comes Morris Townsend (Mr. Clift), a determined, aggressive young man with more than his share of charm and persuasiveness, who dissipated a small inheritance on a European tour, and is now looking to shore up his fortunes. He pursues Catherine, overwhelms her, deceives the naive young woman into believing he loves her for herself alone, and soon they are engaged.

Her father sees through all this, and curtly rebuffs the young adventurer, but Catherine overrules him for once in her life, and plans an elopement despite a trip to Europe with her father that does not deflect her purpose, as her father had hoped.

But when Morris learns that she plans to break with her father and sacrifice the additional $20,000 a year, which he threatens to leave to his clinic, he precipitously jilts her on the night of their elopement. Embittered, she stands up to her father the next day, informs him that she still loves Morris despite his desertion, tells him that he might have

Olivia de Havilland

Montgomery Clift and Olivia de Havilland

Montgomery Clift and Olivia de Havilland

let someone else try to love her, since he himself did not, and adds that when it comes to bitterness and retaliation this is one field in which he will not compare her with her mother. When her father threatens to alter his will, she challenges him to do so, and gets pen and paper, and when he tells her he doesn't wish to disinherit his only child, now that he is in the throes of a fatal illness, but adds that he has no idea what she will do next, she tells him in icy tones, "That's right, father, you'll *never* know —will you!"

Her father dies of lung fever shortly thereafter, leaving her his entire estate, and for the next seven years she lives alone in the mansion in Washington Square, and when she has to pass through the back garden where she and Morris had plighted their troth, she finds herself remembering and mourning her loss. Then one day, her aunt Lavinia (Miriam Hopkins) tells her Morris has returned from Cali-

fornia and wants to see her. After initial hesitation she agrees; he appears, older, moustached, a little worn and beaten, and asks her to believe that his desertion was actuated by the highest motives, that he did not want to see her sacrifice her fortune. She takes this all in, and agrees to another elopement, but when he returns to pick her up he finds the door barred. She listens ecstatically to his frantic banging as she carries the lamp upstairs; revenge has purged her, and she is at peace.

Miss de Havilland is wise and reticent when the occasion calls for it; breathlessly, shatteringly in love while taken in by her delusion; bitter and indeed diabolical when she turns on the father who had for so long held her in contempt; and slyly cat-and-mouse-ish with the returned suitor whose lying duplicities she penetrates only too well. For after seven years her character has taken on dignity, a knowledge of the ways of the world and of men's hearts and minds, and her alert expression and wary glances get this transformation across clearly.

Mr. Clift tightropes gracefully with a character that is devious and given to mendacity, yet almost boyish in its greed and consciousness of the power of its own charm. Money and a life of ease, luxury and irresponsibility are his only life-aims, yet there is almost an innocence in his single-minded pursuit of these regardless of whom he hurts—an innocence whose destructive darker side the old maid of Washington Square no longer feels is worth countenancing and indulging.

Miriam Hopkins is fine indeed, as she always is in a Wyler production, for he had a gift of ferreting out the special alchemies of her mystique, and she responded well to him. Her aunt is solicitous, compassionate, romantic yet realistic, and she feels that Catherine should settle for even a greedy man who offers her the physical and romantic image she would have found fulfilling.

Every scene is precise in its detail, carefully wrought, literately written, painstakingly directed. And what scenes! De Havilland's wondering awakening to love as the unctuous Clift whispers sweet nothings and plays a seductive love tune on the piano; her deep, dark agonies as she waits hour after hour in the drawing-room for her inconstant swain to appear for their elopement; her arresting reversal of character and personality as she wages war with her father for the first time ("At last you have found a tongue, Catherine, if only to say such terrible things to me," Richardson gasps).

The ambivalence in her mood and expression as she listens to Clift's lying reassurances and unctuous insincerities the second time around, after which she tells her aunt, "He came twice—I shall see to it he never comes a third time." For pride in her, after all her disillusionment and humiliation, is stronger than passion, and when her shocked aunt tells her, "Oh how cruel you are, Catherine," she replies crisply, "Yes, I can be very cruel, for I have been taught by masters."

Richardson is a joy to behold—starchy, crisply cynical, supercilious toward the daughter he tolerates but despises, brutal with the young man who comes seeking, honestly amazed when he finds his daughter has a strength of spirit to match his own. Under Wyler's guidance, Richardson chisels out a fine cameo of delicately observed moods and nuances, gestures and expressions, all the way from jingling his keys to laying down his gloves. His speech inflections play like the finest music; his mannerisms are precisely attuned to the emotional currents of the moment. A lifted eyebrow, an impatient gesture, the way he closes a door—all illuminate the character of Dr. Sloper.

The Heiress is romance at its disciplined finest —romance essentially desentimentalized, realistic, aware—yet not without its special brand of mourning tenderness and heartbreak. It is a masterpiece by any yardstick, and one of Wyler's enduring memorials.

Miriam Hopkins and Ralph Richardson

Ralph Richardson and Olivia de Havilland

Montgomery Clift, Olivia de Havilland and Ralph Richardson

155

My Foolish Heart

Samuel Goldwyn-RKO

1950

CREDITS: Directed by Mark Robson. Produced by Samuel Goldwyn. Screenplay by Julius J. and Philip G. Epstein, based on a story by J. D. Salinger. Photographed by Lee Garmes. Music by Victor Young. Song by Victor Young and Ned Washington. Music conducted by Emil Newman. Edited by Daniel Mandell.

OPENED at the Radio City Music Hall, January 19, 1950. Running time: 98 minutes.

CAST: Dana Andrews (Walt Dreiser); Susan Hayward (Eloise Winters); Kent Smith (Lew Wengler); Lois Wheeler (Mary Jane); Jessie Royce Landis (Martha Winters); Robert Keith (Henry Winters); Gigi Perreau (Ramona); Karin Booth (Miriam Ball); Tod Karns (Her Escort); Philip Fine (Sgt. Lucey); Martha Mears (Nightclub Singer); Edna Holland (Dean Whiting); Jerry Paris (Usher); Marietta Canty (Grace); Barbara Woodell (Red Cross Receptionist); Regina Wallace (Mrs. Crandall).

Susan Hayward and Gigi Perreau

Kent Smith and Susan Hayward

Mark Robson, who had made a name for himself as a Hollywood director with two solid 1949 hits, *Champion* and *Home of the Brave*, was offered a change of pace by Samuel Goldwyn and presented with a love story, *My Foolish Heart*, from a screenplay by Julius and Philip G. Epstein based on a J. D. Salinger story. Susan Hayward and Dana Andrews were engaged for the leads, the usual Goldwyn production mounting was enlisted to support Robson's efforts, and Victor Young was commissioned to write the score. Young not only contributed one of his more creditable musical jobs but found he had a hit on his hands in the popular song, "My Foolish Heart" which he wrote with lyricist Ned Washington, and the melodic line of which appears in various arrangements throughout the 98-minute film.

Excellent supporting actors were also hired: Kent Smith Lois Wheeler, Jessie Royce Landis, and Robert Keith, a well-known Broadway character actor (and father of actor Brian Keith) who made his film debut as Hayward's father.

For her work in this film, Susan Hayward won a well-deserved Academy Award nomination as Eloise Winters, the girl who loves a World War II soldier not wisely but too well. Walt Dreiser (Dana Andrews) is a Greenwich Village love-'em-and-leave-'em type when the main story begins in 1941, but he finds college girl Hayward something special and they begin a serious romance cut short by his army service. While he is in training, they continue to meet on his furloughs, and in time they become intimate.

When she learns she is to have a child, she decides not to tell him, especially after her father, Keith, informs her in a moment of rueful reminiscence that he and her mother (Miss Landis), relative strangers to each other at the time, had married in a flash of World War I-style fleeting infatuation and spent the next two decades regretting it.

Andrews is to leave for overseas service and on their last night together, she still withholds the truth. He does not proffer marriage, telling her his future is too uncertain, but adds that her love has meant everything to him. Later he tells her in an undelivered note to come to the base, that he has changed his mind and wants to marry her. She

156

Dana Andrews and Susan Hayward

Dana Andrews and Susan Hayward at right

Lois Wheeler and Susan Hayward

Dana Andrews and Susan Hayward

receives the note after his death in a training accident.

Desolate and bewildered, she accepts the proposal of Kent Smith, the boyfriend of her best pal Lois Wheeler, and though she gives her child a name she condemns herself to seven unhappy years of marriage to a man she does not love while mourning the man she did love.

The picture opens with a cynical, guilt-ridden Hayward, circa 1949, determined to tell her husband that their little girl is not his. Miss Wheeler, who still loves the man she lost to Hayward, visits the house, and Hayward, during a hiatus from a quarrel with Smith, finds in the closet an old dress that takes her back, in a flashback, to reminiscences of a happier time.

At the end of the film, which reverts again to the present, Wheeler persuades Smith, who had planned to declare Hayward an unfit mother because of her drinking and erratic conduct in general, to leave mother and child together and go off with her. She also tells Hayward she forgives her for deflecting Smith's attention for seven years and adds that what happened to her could have happened to anyone.

As Hayward hears the car drive off, she gently strokes the head of the whimpering, delicate child who is the permanent memento of the love she lost.

Of course all this is built-in "women's appeal" stuff—not that there is anything wrong with that—and it would rank as out-and-out soap opera were it not for Hayward and company's fine, sincere acting, the naturalistic approach of director Robson, who demonstrates here that he could be as effective a director of emotion-laden dramas as he was of action and fight epics—and the well-written, often humorous and touching screenplay.

Robert Keith as the anxious father who believes, nonetheless, in children living their own lives, is warm and true in his characterization, and Jessie Royce Landis contributes an outstanding stint as the fussy, flighty mother. Andrews is relaxed, debonair and winning as the man who established his own private and peculiar claim to remembrance and Miss Hayward gets the whole business together in fine style, lending to her role a restrained tenderness and centrifugal force. Romantic the film is, but in an almost naturalistic, underplayed way—and the result is a mature drama of lost love.

The Blue Veil

RKO

1951

CREDITS: Directed by Curtis Bernhardt. An RKO release of a Jerry Wald-Norman Krasna production. Raymond Hakim, Associate Producer. Screenplay by Norman Corwin from a story by François Campaux. Photographed by Frank Planer. Music by Franz Waxman. Music direction by C. Bakaleinikoff. Makeup by Perc Westmore. Edited by George J. Amy.

OPENED at the Criterion Theatre, New York, October 26, 1951. Running time: 113 minutes.

CAST: Jane Wyman (Louise Mason); Charles Laughton (Fred Begley); Joan Blondell (Annie Rawlins); Richard Carlson (Gerald Kean); Don Taylor (Doctor Robert Palfrey); Cyril Cusack (Frank Hutchins); Henry Morgan (Charles Hall); Audrey Totter (Helen Williams); Everett Sloane (District Attorney); Natalie Wood (Stephanie Rawlins); Warner Anderson (Bill Ashworth); Alan Napier (Professor George Carter); Henry Morgan (Mr. Hull); Vivian Vance (Alicia); Les Tremayne (Joplin); John Ridgely (Doctor); Dan O'Herlihy (Williams); Carleton G. Young (Henry Palfrey); Dan Seymour (Pelt).

Charles Laughton, Vivian Vance, Jane Wyman

Jane Wyman, Natalie Wood and Joan Blondell

A warm, tender, unaffected film opened in New York in the fall of 1951. It was devoid of sexual elements, boasted no major love story, deglamorized its heroine—and meandered its humble way into the hearts of millions over the country.

This was *The Blue Veil*, and it contained one of Jane Wyman's more sensitive performances. In it she played a character who seemed to be conducting a platonic romance with the great wide world, especially the children who over the years came under her care as a nursemaid. For that is all she is, from start to finish: a nurse who loves children. In fact, in her old age she is reduced to being a janitress, but that is all right with her, too, for it's in a school where she can be near kids.

It all begins in 1918 when Miss Wyman, a World War I widow, decides to devote her life to children after losing her only child to death. First she works for corset manufacturer Charles Laughton (in one of his quieter, underplayed performances), taking care of his only son. Laughton takes a fancy to her and wants her to marry him, but she isn't in love, and refuses as tactfully as she can. But along comes another woman who *doesn't* refuse him, and the new mistress of the house decides that Wyman must go and that she herself will care for the boy to whom Wyman has grown deeply attached. This sets her off on peregrinations to asorted domiciles, all of them with children.

At the home of wealthy Agnes Moorehead she meets tutor Richard Carlson, who is more the kind of man she wants to make a life with, but he is an uncertain, indecisive soul who gets cold feet when they are about to elope, and she is free as air again.

She then finds herself caring for the neglected daughter (Natalie Wood) of ambitious, preoccupied comedy performer Joan Blondell, but when she realizes that Blondell will lose her daughter's love if

With Cyril Cusack

Jane Wyman and Don Taylor

Richard Carlson and Jane Wyman

Jane Wyman and Richard Carlson

Jane Wyman, Vivian Vance and Charles Laughton

she isn't alerted, she sacrifices young Miss Wood to her true mother with the same unselfish spirit with which she has surrendered the other children.

Shortly she is caring for a little boy abandoned by his mother, and she grows particularly attached to this child over a period of years—but the mother (Audrey Totter) comes back unexpectedly from England with a new husband (Henry Morgan) and forces the District Attorney to demand the boy's return. In one of the film's more moving scenes, Miss Wyman asks the District Attorney if the restored parent will ever know all the little things about that boy that she knows, having nursed him through

Jane Wyman and Charles Laughton

assorted illnesses and watched him grow, and the official (Everett Sloane in one of his better performances) forced by his position and the law to turn the boy over to Totter and Morgan, expresses his disgust with the pair and his admiration for Wyman.

Wyman grows older, and younger women supersede her as nursemaids. She runs up against a coolly officious employment specialist who tells her bluntly she is now superannuated for the job she loves. When asked what else she will take, Wyman replies, "Anything near children." Reduced to a janitress job in a public school, she sits sadly in the middle of a shoddy classroom, broom forgotten, after a little boy she has attempted to embrace runs in unthinking childish disgust from her gray hair and wrinkles.

Finally she encounters a doctor, Don Taylor, who turns out to be one of the boys she had cared for, and he surprises her with a party at which many of her "children" turn up. And for a heart-tug she gets to talk on the phone to the boy she loved most of

all, now far away with his family. Taylor and his wife present the old lady with their two young children and inform her that she is to care for them and live in their house always.

If the story sounds sentimental in the extreme, it was. It was also deeply moving as mounted and presented, and we defy you, the next time it shows up on TV, to withhold sympathetic tears as Miss Wyman, a past mistress at this sort of thing, assaults your emotions on at least a dozen occasions during the 113-minute running time. (If TV cuts it, don't blame us.)

She also had the benefit of the prescient Curtis Bernhardt's direction, a literate Norman Corwin screenplay from a Francois Campaux story, fine photography by Frank Planer and one of composer Franz Waxman's most poignant scores.

Truly Jane Wyman's romance with the world, *The Blue Veil* belongs among the Great Romantic Films as much as any picture we can think of. Many are the ways of love.

Rhapsody

Metro-Goldwyn-Mayer

1954

CREDITS: Directed by Charles Vidor. Produced by Lawrence Weingarten. Screenplay by Fay and Michael Kanin based on an adaptation by Ruth and Augustus Goetz of the novel *Maurice Guest* by Henry Handel Richardson. Photographed by Robert Planck. Musical adaptation by Bronislau Kaper. Musical and orchestral direction by Johnny Green. Art Directors, Cedric Gibbons and Paul Groesse. Set decorations by Edwin B. Willis and Hugh Hunt. Montage sequences by Peter Ballbusch. Sound by Douglas Shearer. Technicolor consultant, Alvord Eiseman. Edited by John Dunning. Gowns by Helen Rose. Hairstyles by Sydney Guilaroff. Makeup by William Tuttle. Piano supervision, Harold Gelman. Violin Supervision, Morris Brenner. MGM Symphony Orchestra. Michael Rabin played the Tchaikovsky "Violin Concerto in D Major"; Claudio Arrau played Rachmaninoff's "Second Piano Concerto in C Minor."

OPENED at Radio City Music Hall, March 11, 1954. Running time: 115 minutes.

CAST: Elizabeth Taylor (Louise Durant); Vittorio Gassman (Paul Brontë); John Ericson (James Guest); Louis Calhern (Nicholas Durant); Michael Chekhov (Professor Schuman); Barbara Bates (Effie Cahill); Richard Hageman (Bruno Furst); Richard Lupino (Otto Kraft); Celia Lovsky (Frau Sigerlist); Stuart Whitman (Student); Madge Blake (Mrs. Cahill); Jack Raine (Edmund Streller); Brigit Nielsen (Madeleine); Jacqueline Duval (Yvonne); Norman Nevens (Student Pianist).

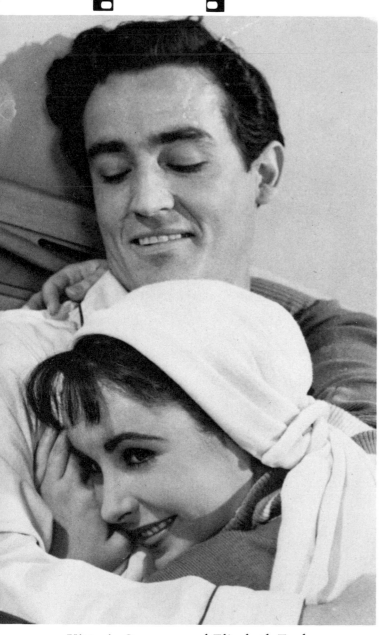

Vittorio Gassman and Elizabeth Taylor

" 'I must possess the man I love, heart, body and soul'; Elizabeth Taylor as a woman obsessed with insatiable desire!" That's what MGM's ad copy screamed during its tub-thumping for *Rhapsody*, and Miss Taylor, in what I consider the best performance of her now-thirty-year film career, lived up to every word of it in this florid romance of a girl who had too much money and beauty for her own good, and two musicians who react according to their individual natures to her emotional demands.

I have never had too high an opinion of Miss Taylor's basic talents, her two Oscars notwithstanding. Cinematically she is ideal, in a visual and personality sense, but her exceptional beauty and potent sexual chemistry have too long disguised the fact that her spirit is more that of a kitten than a tigress, her basic emotions immature despite all she has gone through in real life, and her outlook on life shallow and girlish rather than deep and womanly. She meows when she should roar, and she is petulant when she should be angry, she is sentimental when she should be tragically emotional, and she is rasping when she should be authentically tough-grained. Her first Oscar-winner, *Butterfield 8* (1960) was for a mediocre performance in a role that should have gone to Susan Hayward or someone equally authoritative and brittle; her second award was for *Who's Afraid of Virginia Woolf* (1966) and *that* should have gone to Bette Davis, who, fifty-eight or no fifty-eight, comprehended the subtle malevolences and self-flagellations of the Albee character far better than Miss Taylor at thirty-four—or any age.

But in *Rhapsody*, filmed when she was twenty-one, Miss Taylor was a true a*ctress* as she has often been a genuine *star*—and why? Because the part had met the woman, or girl, rather. Miss Taylor's shallow emotional makeup and limited intellectual capacity identified, and meshed, perfectly with Louise Durant, a not very bright but ravishingly sexy heiress peregrinating around Europe mooning over a handsome violinist who, being more mature, bright, and more

Elizabeth Taylor and Vittorio Gassman

gifted and dedicated, eventually gave short shrift to her whining possessiveness and constant demands for attention. Vittorio Gassman as Paul Brontë, the violinist, is a lively guy who likes his wine and women as much as any man but when work is called for, he *works*—and ravishing Miss Taylor and everybody else had better get out of the way. Of course she can't take this, and when she sees him driving off with another girl who plays it slightly cooler, it's off to the medicine cabinet and the sleeping pills.

As her cynical socialite father (Louis Calhern in one of his more ingratiating roles) tells her: "My dear, you have a neurotic need to be needed, and your Mr. Brontë obviously needs no one—except his violin, of course."

But it seems there's a shy, sensitive, self-de-precating, and insecure young man upstairs in the Zurich lodging house and he is equally as talented on the piano as Mr. Gassman is on the violin, and he *does* need Miss Taylor. John Ericson plays James Guest, the musician who rescues Miss Taylor from suicide in the knick of time. Listlessly she settles (for a time) into a rebound relationship with him while Gassman fiddles his way to increasing fame, but finally she wants out and icily informs Ericson, "You can get over anything!" "Can you," he flares, and flips on the radio to a Gassman concert which has her faltering and languishing again soon enough —and so they get married.

But Miss Taylor is not the kind of woman any ambitious artist should be married to, and knowing that she doesn't love him and only went along with

Vittorio Gassman and Elizabeth Taylor

his love for *her* for lack of anything better to do, Mr. Ericson takes to drink and living off her money, his promising pianistic career forgotten.

Her path again crosses Gassman's in Paris, but when he sees what her destructiveness has done to his fellow artist he again scorns her. She is then shocked into doing something constructive for a change, and drags her wondering young husband back to the Zurich conservatory, and whereas before she had regarded the violinist's work as a rival, she treats her husband's blossoming career as if it were her own, not his, keeping him practicing, stopping up her ears when all the scales get too much for her, and dreaming only of the day she can show her violinist he was wrong about her.

Finally comes the night of her husband's concert—he is to play the "Second Piano Concerto" of Rachmaninoff (incidentally the most overworked classical piece in all cinematic repertory)—and a delighted Gassman, who has gotten wind of the event via a note sent by her father, is on hand to whisk her away now that she has proven her—or rather her husband's—mettle.

But lo and behold (and as if you didn't know)

John Ericson. Richard Hageman conducting

she gets so emotionally worked-up watching her young husband suffering and sweating his way through the concerto (after she has just told him he doesn't need her any more and that she is going off with Gassman) that it is apparent to her watching swain as well as everyone else that now it is her husband she loves. And so she sends the violinist away, goes to her husband, who is fingering his piano wistfully later on an empty stage (he was a smash success, of course) and tells him all fools need luck and will he take her back? Which he does joyfully, to a crescendo musical finish.

That, then, is the story of *Rhapsody*, and it makes surprisingly effective romantic cinema. First off, it points a good moral: to wit, people should accept their responsibilities to others as well as to themselves, and true happiness comes from accentuating *giving*, not *taking*. Then it is lushly mounted, with handsome settings, top production values, literate writing, Miss Taylor in her best performance, Vittorio Gassman his most charming self, and sensitive, luminous John Ericson in *his* finest work. Ericson is another actor whose unusual talent and mystique have been grossly neglected by Hollywood, as were John Kerr's and others. Here he gets across an interesting synthesis of manly amiability and fierce tenderness, making his characterization of an essentially dependent and affectionate person who rises to the demands of his artistry when called upon, a rather affecting and memorable incarnation.

Calhern and other character actors lend sterling support, especially Michael Chekhov, who makes something special of his music-professor role.

Barbara Bates, Elizabeth Taylor and Vittorio Gassman

Then there is Johnny Green's excellent musical direction, the fine renditions by Michael Rabin's violin of Tchaikovsky's violin concerto and other works; the expert playing of Claudio Arrau, who keeps that Rachmaninoff piece singing, and Peter Ballbusch's montage work, which whips around Europe in fine, elegant, fast-paced style.

Rhapsody is a romance that makes one think; it has a moral; it is beautifully mounted, Miss Taylor, besides looking ravishing, gives a *performance* in a role she *understands*; it has a fine and unusual ending that leaves one glowing—and when revived on TV it proves that twenty years have not diminished its impact and its radiant verve and affirmation.

Elizabeth Taylor, John Ericson and Louis Calhern

**All
That
Heaven
Allows**

**Universal-
International**

1956

CREDITS: Directed by Douglas Sirk. Produced by Ross Hunter. Production Manager, Sergei Petschnikoff. Screenplay by Peg Fenwick. From a story by Edna Lee and Harry Lee. Photographed by Russell Metty. Art Direction by Alexander Golitzen and Eric Orbom. Sets designed by Russell A. Gausman and Julie Heron. Music by Frank Skinner and Joseph Gershenson. Costumes by Bill Thomas. Dialogue Director, Jack Daniels. Color by Technicolor. Color Consultant, William Fritzsche.

OPENED at the Mayfair Theatre, New York, February 28, 1956. Running time: 89 minutes.

CAST: Jane Wyman (Cary Scott); Rock Hudson (Ron Kirby); Agnes Moorehead (Sara Warren); Conrad Nagel (Harvey); Virginia Grey (Alida Anderson); Gloria Talbott (Kay Scott); William Reynolds (Ned Scott); Jacqueline de Wit (Mona Plash); Charles Drake (Mick Anderson); Leigh Snowden (Jo-Ann); Merry Anders (Mary Ann); Donald Curtis (Howard Hoffer); Alex Gerry (George Warren).

Jane Wyman and Virginia Grey

Jane Wyman and Rock Hudson

Director Douglas Sirk, one of Hollywood's more underrated talents, said in a recent interview that he had directed the 1956 Universal film, *All That Heaven Allows,* in the spirit of his literary idols Henry David Thoreau and Ralph Waldo Emerson, the 19th century New England writers who counseled individualism. He particularly had in mind, he said, Thoreau's injunction that if a man does not keep pace with his fellows, because he hears a different drummer, he should obey that which he hears, however measured and far away. This paraphrase of a famous aphorism expresses the spirit of this fine picture as well as anything could.

For here we have another film masterpiece, underrated, misunderstood and passed over in its own time as "just another soap opera." It was hardly that, with its penetrating, literate screenplay by Peg Fenwick, based on a story by Edna Lee and Harry Lee; its tasteful sets and artwork; the care taken in its execution in all departments, and the musical direction of Frank Skinner and Joseph Gershenson, who cleverly adapted some of the finest music of Franz Liszt and other romantic composers to fit the film's action.

And not only was the film exquisitely tooled, carefully thought out, it was also invested (thanks, we suspect, mainly to director Sirk) with emotional power and romantic exaltation. A perfect blend of fine, sympathetic acting (by stars Rock Hudson, Jame Wyman and Agnes Moorehead, Virginia Grey, and others) and able craftsmanship in other principal departments, *All That Heaven Allows* has been frequently revived on television, where it has the strange knack of looking fresh and new with each viewing.

The film is also beautifully photographed in Technicolor, catching the change of seasons in the New England town where it is supposedly set in an enchanting blend of colors and shadings.

Among other things, this cinematic treasure is a mature study of middle-aged loneliness and the refusal to surrender the heart's dearest hopes to conformist, muddled life-patterns.

Jane Wyman is a widow in a small town who is having difficulty in adjusting to her status. Middle-aged, with children at college, she lives in comfortable circumstances in a handsome house, but avoids shallow socializing and the foolish pursuits of her snobbish set to live and dream reclusively in her home, waiting for she knows not what.

Rock Hudson and Jane Wyman

Jane Wyman, Virginia Grey, Charles Drake and Rock Hudson

Conrad Nagel, Agnes Moorehead, Jane Wyman and Alex Gerry

A young gardener, Rock Hudson, comes to prune her trees, and she is strangely drawn to him. An idealist and nonconformist, he prefers to grow plants in his nursery near an old mill, and live life according to his own rules—which do not comprise cocktail parties, gossip, shallow camaraderie with the mediocrities of the town, or the coarser varieties of roistering. He is obviously all-man, however, and she gives herself numerous reasons why she should not encourage him, the difference in their respective ages being, in her view, the most salient of all. But he keeps returning, it is obvious he is attracted to her, and when he takes her to visit his friends she is enchanted by their refusal to let unimportant things become important, their adherence to Rousseau's concepts of individualism and personal integrity and their scorn of the commercialistc rat-race.

But as their romance deepens, so does the widow's dilemma, and when she encounters the opposition of her social set, and the disgusted reactions of her two children, she retreats, and leaves the man she loves and who loves her for the death-in-life she had known before.

But the grown children who insist that she maintain their family image leave her for lives of their own, her loneliness deepens and she asks herself: was it worth the sacrifice?

The family doctor, whom she consults on her "headaches," tells her they are purely psychosomatic, that there is nothing wrong with her. "Marry him," he tells her. "Stop running away. Stop living by the opinions, the smiles and frowns of others." He adds, "You were ready for a love affair but you weren't ready for love."

And so the widow goes to find her young man once more. He is wounded in a fall down an embankment while trying to attract her attention; she has a bad time of it when it looks as though he won't survive. But comes the dawn, in the living room of the old mill he had converted as a home for them, and she is told he will live after all, and promises never to leave him. A deer frolics freely in the snow outside the picture window.

Soapy? Fustian? Women's picture-ish? That's what some of the 1956 critics said. And I suspect part of the picture's troubles with the reviewers were due to the conformist, smug atmosphere of the Eisenhower era when Americans didn't question their basic values and the American dream sent out alarums to the "go-getters" and "regular guys." In the more individualistic, more hospitable world of 1974, the film, which in essence is a paean to individualism and spiritual freedom, just as director Sirk has indicated, is better received when revived. In fact, it seems ahead of its time.

Miss Wyman and Mr. Hudson gave simple, sincere performances, restrained but romantic. As Ralph Waldo Emerson said, "Trust thyself; every heart vibrates to that iron string." *All That Heaven Allows* obviously trusts itself. That is why it is one of the few films in which producer Ross Hunter can take honest pride.

Rock Hudson and Jane Wyman

Rock Hudson and Jane Wyman

Tea and Sympathy

Metro-Goldwyn-Mayer

1956

CREDITS: Directed by Vincente Minnelli. Produced by Pandro S. Berman. Screenplay by Robert Anderson, based on his stage play. Photographed by John Alton. Art Direction by William A. Horning and Edward Carfago. Music by Adolph Deutsch. Edited by Ferris Webster. CinemaScope. MetroColor.

OPENED at Radio City Music Hall, New York, September 27, 1956. Running time: 122 minutes.

CAST: Deborah Kerr (Laura Reynolds); John Kerr (Tom Lee); Leif Erickson (Bill Reynolds); Edward Andrews (Herb Lee); Darryl Hickman (Al); Norma Crane (Ellie Martin); Dean Jones (Ollie); Jacqueline de Wit (Lily Sears); Tom Loughlin (Ralph); Ralph Votrain (Steve); Steven Terrell (Phil); Kip King (Ted); Jimmy Hayes (Henry); Richard Tyler (Roger); Don Burnett (Vic); Mary Alan Hokanson (Mary Williams); Ron Kennedy (Dick); Peter Miller (Pete); Bob Alexander (Pat); Michael Monroe (Earle); Byron Kane (Umpire); Harry Harvey Jr. (first boy); Bobby Ellis (second boy); Saul Gorss, Dale Van Sickle (Burly men); Peter Leeds (Headmaster at bonfire); Del Erickson (Ferdie).

Deborah Kerr and John Kerr

Leif Erickson, Deborah Kerr and Edward Andrews

When Robert Anderson was assigned by Metro-Goldwyn-Mayer to do the screen version of his affecting and perceptive play, *Tea and Sympathy*, he informed one and all that there would be no tampering with the basic theme, that its integrity would be preserved, and its message put across to the film public with the same uncompromising force with which it had been unleashed on the theatre-going public. He succeeded in his intentions, making only minor changes (he cut some of the rougher epithets, vulgarisms, name-callings, etc., added scenes at a pajama bonfire and at the town prostitute's, innuendoed some of the play's more glaring assertions).

Nonetheless the basic message of *Tea and Sympathy* came across on screen as forcefully as on stage—that particularly meretricious examples of man's inhumanity to man can be found in boys' schools, where boy's inhumanity to boy is often a reflection of the obtuse attitudes and benighted shibboleths of their cravenly conformist elders.

Deborah Kerr and John Kerr, who had starred together in the 1953 theatre piece, a smash Broadway hit of that season, were reunited for the film, and an eloquent and persuasive pair they made. Considering all the times they had played it on Broadway, their portrayals had a freshness, an emotional immediacy and a deeply touching element that constituted ensemble playing at its finest, the rest of the ensemble, Leif Erickson and Edward Andrews among others, complementing them ably.

The story deals with Tom Lee, poor at sports (except tennis), fond of music, given to wearing his hair long, addicted to romantic dreaming while the other boys are engaged in athletic competition. He is suspected of being "unmasculine," and proves an embarrassment to his well-meaning but conformist roommate (Darryl Hickman) and a pariah figure to the other prep school boys at one of those fashionable Eastern establishments.

He is held in contempt by his housemaster, Leif Erickson, a more complex man than his hearty surface would indicate. His father (Edward Andrews) worries, too, about his masculinity, and keeps counseling him to get his hair cut, "get into shape" with his fellows, and redeem the hard-won family image.

His only true friend is Laura (Deborah Kerr), the housemaster's wife, who finds that the forlorn eighteen-year-old reminds her strangely of her first husband, a sensitive young man who went to war to "prove" his manhood and got killed for his pains.

Tom arouses the added suspicions of his cloddish associates when he is discovered sewing with the faculty wives on the beach—an innocent skill he acquired from a woman servant his father had left him with in boyhood. Tensions accumulate, his ostracism grows more complete, he is scheduled for a sadistic hazing at a pajama bonfire, his frantic father demands that he "put up a fight," and Laura grows more concerned.

Her husband, alternating between indulgence, exasperation and secret jealousy of Laura's concern

Deborah Kerr, Edward Andrews and Leif Erickson

for Tom, keeps reminding her that her only communicative function is the dispensing of "tea and sympathy" on Sunday afternoons, but step by step Laura and Tom are drawn close, and when she tries to stop his visit to the town prostitute, which he plans in a desperate effort to "prove his manhood," and he turns to her for love, her standards demand that she push him away. Whereupon he rushes to the prostitute.

His visit proves a fiasco, and he attempts suicide. Later he disappears, and Laura overhears her husband and his father discussing his "failure." In a confrontation with her ever-more-preoccupied and essentially unloving and neglectful husband, she tells him that it wasn't just "sympathy," but her heart in its loneliness crying out to the boy for the comfort he could give her as well as himself.

But her husband, who is obviously rigidly suppressing his own homosexual impulses and hates the innocent Tom for appearing to symbolize it (and hence is unwittingly a threat), turns away from her, and aware that he has nothing more to give her, neither consolation nor understanding, nor love, she goes to find the despairing Tom, overtakes him in a wood, and with the famous words, "When you speak of this in future years—and you will—be kind," she gives herself to him.

Miss Kerr gives perhaps the best performance of her career in *Tea and Sympathy*. She is wise, womanly, compassionate, consummately eloquent in scene after scene: attempting to persuade her husband that for Tom, it has to be love, whereas for many other boys sex is merely coarse, impersonal animalism, agonizing over her inability to save Tom from the prostitute after he has fled her living room into the rain; grieving over her one-sided love for her floundering, self-deceiving husband, pleading with Tom's father to give him understanding.

John Kerr, a fine and sensitive actor who never seemed to make it in subsequent films, is also in top form, in a role tailored to his measure. He is utterly convincing as a tormented eighteen-year-old despite the fact he was twenty-four when he did the film. The failure of Hollywood producers to build him into a star through carefully chosen, distinctive roles of the kind in which he could have flourished is just another example of the shortsightedness of the era in which he came to fleeting prominence.

Leif Erickson, an actor of considerably more depth and range than his usual Hollywood stereotype-casting would indicate, is superb as Bill Reynolds, Laura's housemaster spouse, and Edward Andrews gets across all the cloddish bewilderment of a man who lives only for the opinions of others.

On the 1956 screen *Tea and Sympathy* came as a revelation. It was so much more penetrating and psychologically perceptive than most films of the year that it shocked audiences as much as it moved them. Even in the far more liberated and individualistic atmosphere of 1974, when prep-school boys deify individualism above conformity, wear their hair long, and show each other more tolerance, *Tea and Sympathy* retains all of its bite and impact. It is a terrifying study of adolescent loneliness and bewilderment. It is also a compassionate study of the infinite resources of the heart, and the boundless capacity for true compassion that resides in some of us.

The film itself, expertly directed by Vincente Minnelli, speaks for all the sorrow-laden, persecuted, unwanted "off-horses" of all times and all environments. As such it is a superb exposition of bitter truths, and a compassionate preachment against man's inhumanity to man.

Deborah Kerr
and John Kerr

The Barretts of Wimpole Street

Metro-Goldwyn-Mayer

1957

CREDITS: Directed by Sidney Franklin. Produced by Sam Zimbalist. Screenplay by John Dighton from the play by Rudolf Besier. MetroColor and CinemaScope. Music by Bronislau Kaper. Song: "Wilt Thou Have My Hand" by Herbert Stothart. Photographed by F. A. Young. Art direction by Alfred Junge. Photographic effects by Tom Howard. Recording supervision by A. W. Watkins. Costumes by Elizabeth Haffenden. Production manager, Dora Wright. Color Consultant, John Bridge.

OPENED at Radio City Music Hall, January 17, 1957. Running time: 105 minutes.

CAST: Jennifer Jones (Elizabeth Barrett); John Gielgud (Edward Moulton Barrett); Bill Travers (Robert Browning); Virginia McKenna (Henrietta); Susan Stephen (Bella); Vernon Gray (Captain Surtees Cook); Jean Anderson (Wilson); Maxine Audley (Arabel); Leslie Phillips (Harry Bevan); Laurence Naismith (Doctor Chambers); Moultrie Kelsall (Doctor Ford Waterlow); Michael Brill (George); Kenneth Fortescue (Octavius); Nicholas Hawtrey (Henry); Richard Thorp (Alfred); Keith Baxter (Charles); Brian Smith (Septimus). And Flush, a spaniel.

Virginia McKenna and Jennifer Jones

The Barretts of Wimpole Street has passed through three successive incarnations. In 1931 it was a celebrated play with Katharine Cornell. It was one of Miss Cornell's most-loved portrayals, and during World War II she toured it at military posts all over the world. In 1934 Irving Thalberg purchased it for MGM as a vehicle for his wife Norma Shearer, and she and Fredric March (as Browning) and Charles Laughton (as Edward Moulton Barrett) enjoyed great success with it.

In 1957 the second film version appeared, and it was superior to the first on a number of counts. This costarred Jennifer Jones as Elizabeth Barrett, Bill Travers as Robert Browning and Sir John Gielgud as Edward Moulton Barrett, in handsome CinemaScope and color, which the 1934 version did not boast, and replete with rich, moving theme music which the earlier version lacked—a strange oversight, considering Irving Thalberg's perfectionism and director Sidney Franklin's thoroughness.

The 1957 version had also the benefit of Bill Travers's manly, robust, forceful Robert Browning, one of this underrated and overlooked actor's more notable achievements, and though Miss Jones was not up to Miss Shearer's standard, she acquitted herself creditably. But the surprise of the picture was Gielgud, who filled the Edward Moulton Barrett character with subtle diabolism and rich complexities born as much of the Gielgud genius as of the original Barrett's mystique, which, from all reports, was baleful enough. I have always considered this the finest of many fine Gielgud performances on stage and screen; something in the character met something in the man and artist, and the result was a portrayal that rated at least an Academy Award nomination (but unfortunately didn't get it).

There was also a more authentic look to the 1957 version, shot as it was in England, in handsome settings and exterior shots that far outranked for verisimilitude and correct atmosphere the Hollywood conceptions of 1934. The cast, all English except for Miss Jones, seemed also to fit more truly into every Barrett-Browning aficionado's concept of the time, the place and the people of this immortal story.

Jennifer Jones and John Gielgud

John Gielgud

*Laurence Naismith, Jennifer Jones and
Jean Anderson*

Bill Travers, John Gielgud and Jennifer Jones

Sidney Franklin, who directed both versions, improved distinctly on his original work, fine as that was, helped possibly by the advantages cited above, and John Dighton's screenplay from the Rudolf Besier play was literate, tasteful and right in tune with the ambience.

The famous story needs only a cursory recapitulation, since it is known by now to almost every literate person: Elizabeth Barrett, delicate in health, robust in her poetic outpourings, is confined to her quarters in her father's London home, circa 1845, her books, her dog, her faithful attendant Wilson, and the occasional visits from her father and family her only outlets. Lonely and spiritually desolate for all her courage and surface gaiety, she has resigned herself permanently to the loss of love, a drab, limited existence, and an early death. Then into her life comes the live-loving, life-affirming poet Robert Browning, and her being is revitalized, her health improves, she rises from her couch into the sunlight of a confident and reciprocated love. Her angered father, a tyrant who rules his brood with a sadistic ferocity, and cherishes a special predilection for his daughter Elizabeth, counters Browning's liberative efforts at every turn, and disguises his selfish possessiveness under a pseudo-religiosity, Victorian-style.

Finally, when she realizes the incestuous nature of her father's fixation on her, she leaves his house forever and marries Browning, who for months has been passionately urging just such a step. When her father reads her parting note, he attempts to have her beloved dog, Flush, destroyed, but one of the other children tells him she has taken the pet with her. Whereupon his shoulders slump in a final defeat, though from all indications he will continue to rule his Wimpole Street brood with an iron hand.

Virginia McKenna is splendid as Henrietta, who is forced by her father to promise she will never again see the young man she loves; she disobeys him, and glories in the bible "oath" she broke, having heeded Miss Jones' injunction to follow the dictates of her own heart. Michael Brill, Kenneth Fortescue, Richard Thorp, Keith Baxter, Nicholas Hawtrey and Brian Smith are as true to their 1845 young-Victorian ambience as any daguerreotype could reveal, and Jean Anderson makes a warm and compassionate Wilson.

The picture contains many touching scenes: Elizabeth's first, painful, tentative move from her couch-prison to struggle, step by step, to the window to watch Browning leave after his first visit, the superbly contrapuntal cross-emotion of her final struggle with her father, her humorous badinage with Browning at their first meeting, their love scene amidst the flowers of the park, his delight when she walks downstairs to greet him at a subsequent visit, her wistful expression as she listens to a cousin plan a wedding.

Jennifer Jones and John Gielgud

Bill Travers and Jennifer Jones

I have always held Jennifer Jones in higher esteem than most film critics seem to do; I feel she is not an Oscar-winning actress (for 1943's *Song of Bernadette*) for nothing, and I have found her performances in a variety of roles, from the sultry, sexy *Ruby Gentry* to the ethereal waif in *Portrait of Jennie*, indicative of considerable depth, range and virtuosity. If she is not quite up to Norma Shearer's standard in the earlier *Barretts* it is largely because the beautiful and talented Miss Shearer was chemically and pictorially more right for the role. Here Miss Jones is charming, often touching, and dynamic and fiery enough when the occasion calls for it. And in her scenes opposite one of the world's greatest actors (and scene-snatchers), Gielgud, she holds her own very well. As for Bill Travers, he should have been launched on a major film career with his Browning portrayal, but wasn't. Strange are the ways of the movie industry.

One of the great romances of all time, *The Barretts of Wimpole Street* reaffirms the healing psychodynamics of love. Its basic mystique is fitting-ly captured in the 1957 film, which for pace, power, emotional content and dynamic spiritual force is one of the best in its category.

Virginia McKenna, Jennifer Jones and John Gielgud

The Roman Spring of Mrs. Stone

Warner Bros.-Seven Arts

1961

CREDIT: Directed by Jose Quintero. Produced by Louis De Rochemont. A Seven Arts Presentation. Screenplay by Gavin Lambert. Adapted from the novel by Tennessee Williams. Music by Richard Addinsell. Photographed by Harry Waxman. Gowns by Balmain of Paris. Technicolor.

OPENED at the Capitol and Trans-Lux 85th Street Theatres, New York, December 28, 1961. Running time: 104 minutes.

CAST: Vivien Leigh (Karen Stone); Warren Beatty (Paolo); Lotte Lenya (The Contessa); Coral Browne (Meg); Jill St. John (Barbara); Jeremy Spenser (Young Man); Stella Bonheur (Mrs. Jamison-Walker); Josephine Bron (Lucia); Carl Jaffe (Baron); Cleo Laine (Singer); and Bessie Love, Harold Kasket, Peter Dyneley.

Warren Beatty and Vivien Leigh

When the film version of Tennessee Williams's only novel, *The Roman Spring of Mrs. Stone*, was released in late 1961, it weathered a barrage of obtusely unfair reviews. It was damned as "thin" and "bloodless" and "unwholesome" and "tiresome." It was castigated as falsely romanticized tripe about a middle-aged American woman awash amidst the gigolos of Rome, termed "unedifying" and "dreary," and one critic asked why anyone would honestly care about such a woman and her spiritual dilemmas.

Perhaps some 1961 American reviewers didn't care—or understand, for that matter. What they saw was over their heads, beyond their comprehension, and reflective of their lack of worldly experience. Esthetic and spiritual myopics, unfortunately, thrive in all eras.

In 1974 more discerning buffs, film writers and TV viewers have become aware that *The Roman Spring of Mrs. Stone* is something of a minor masterpiece. Here we have showcased the forty-eight-year-old Vivien Leigh playing an American stage actress of fifty who finds herself suddenly widowed. Simultaneously she has discovered that her fast-fading looks will no longer sustain a theatrical career that depended largely on her romantic image. Listlessly she settles in Rome, and aimlessly she wanders about, lost in a brooding reclusiveness, a grayish anomie.

At fifty her past parades before her eyes—a sort of preview of the inner recapitulations of experience the legends insist will haunt us all before our individual deaths—and she asks herself: what is lacking? Since her nature is intrinsically shallow, selfish and brittle, Mrs. Stone not only fails to come up with the correct answers to her inner dilemmas but eventually is destroyed in the search—truly an example of the apothegm: "Character is Fate."

Nonetheless, this woman, for all her shortcomings and character flaws, qualifies as a romantically tragic figure, for she shares with all humankind the need for love, the consolations of beauty, peace, spiritual grace—and these she is denied. She illustrates in the method of her search, the quality of her yearnings, "that great task laid upon a soul unequal to the performance of it."

Though the screenplay varied from Williams's original in some respects, it retained in undiluted strength the sadness and reflectiveness of his highly individual philosophy. With his usual gossamer obliqueness, Williams was feelingfully evocative and autobiographical in spirit here, as he was in his better works for the theatre, and his mystique—its forlorn idealism, its poetic disillusion, its ever-recurring preoccupation with those creatures crippled of soul who are condemned to live in the world's Outer Darknesses—pervades the film as it did the novel.

Miss Leigh at that juncture in her offscreen life found herself quite attuned to Williams's spirit and intentions. At forty-eight her beauty, like Mrs. Stone's, was largely faded; she had just lost her

Vivien Leigh and Warren Beatty

husband of twenty years, Laurence Olivier, who had divorced her to marry a younger woman. She was privately depleted in spirit, rootless in her personal life, and subconsciously she was probably already in a state of preparation for the death that was to overtake her within a scant six years.

For these and other reasons, Miss Leigh's performance in this film was one of her finest, a true product of her disillusioned artistic maturity. It was deeply felt, consciously disciplined and aptly focalized under the discerning, sensitive touch of director Jose Quintero, an old hand at delineating tragic life-situations and tragic human beings.

Warren Beatty gave what I still consider his best performance as Paolo, the young Italian aristocrat turned gigolo, a ruthless narcissist rendered irredeemably cynical by childhood sufferings during World War II. He is a predator and revenge-seeker who senses that in Mrs. Stone he has a subconsciously amenable victim. Beatty had personally pleaded with Williams for the role. He mastered an adept Italian accent and got inside the gigolo's psyche with an uncanny perception. It remains one of the interesting oddities of screen acting that he was never again so subtly fine. The explanation might be that the sensuality, the slyness, the predatory, feel-for-the-soft-spots insensitivity and atavism of Paolo had in them elements akin to aspects of Beatty's private nature. And in this one film in which he displayed himself an artist, they served Beatty well.

As the procuress Contessa who engineers the meeting of Mrs. Stone and Paolo, Lotte Lenya was a revelation, delivering a serpentine, sinuous blend of sophisticated *Weltschmerz* and killer-instinct diabolism in a sharply etched portrait of a cruel and unfeeling female pimp with a stiletto out for the jugular vein. Unctuously she strokes her overfed cat; laughing inwardly with feline craftiness, she reassures a female and a male client. ("I will be able to help you very soon, Madame, but for you, Baron, it will take a little longer.") In one unforgettable scene in a posh, smoky Rome nightclub, Mrs. Stone

181

Warren Beatty and Vivien Leigh

and her boy Paolo sit languidly watching the goings-on. When she sends Paolo for cigarettes, the Contessa slithers over to put the touch on her for providing the original introduction to her inamorata, and the two worldly, aging women, the one so forlornly vulnerable yet defensively brittle still, the other an old hand at ripping up one of Williams's "tender-young-turtle undersides" engage in a feline verbal tournament terrible in its understatement, slashing yet icily restrained.

And when the Contessa, whose greed has not been sufficiently assuaged by the sum Mrs. Stone pays her, takes her revenge by foisting on the vain Paolo a young Hollywood actress (Jill St. John) who promptly steals him from his infatuated patroness, Mrs. Stone's despair is stark indeed. For she has made the mistake of falling deeply in love with Paolo, who scorns her because earlier, in her tactless self-centeredness, she had poked fun at his new white suit. When he seeks to torment her by relating the case of an aging woman found in bed with her throat cut, she trumps his ace with the rejoinder: "After three more years, a cut throat would be a convenience."

Earlier she had cynically told the Contessa: "The beautiful make their own laws," and now she finds that Paolo is truly a law unto himself. And when, goaded beyond endurance, she screams out to Paolo her jealousy of the younger women with whom he dallies, he turns on her savagely with the words, "Rome is 3000 years old—how old are *you*, fifty?" She follows him then to the young actress's hotel and when her worst suspicions are bleakly confirmed, she goes home, takes Paolo's photograph out of its frame and crumples it, puts her house keys in a lace handkerchief, goes to the window and throws them down to a strange, maniacal young man who has been following her in the streets, and who for months has stood by a fountain beneath her window making weird, sinister gestures.

Then she sits in her drawing-room—calm, resigned. Jaded despair triumphant in her face and bearing, all illusions fled, she lights a cigarette and watches in fascination as the young maniac, functioning as her private Angel of Death (or Fiend of Death, rather) slowly crosses the room toward his victim, his dark, watchful, shifting eyes gradually widening, to effect what is in reality her suicide, his coat eventually filling the screen, dissolving it in a final blackness.

For this cynical, bittersweet, well-nigh-perfect example of the "Decadent-Romantic" film, composer Richard Addinsell provided one of his most sensitive and eloquently apposite scores. His music captures all the haunted sorrow, the chilling sense of age vitiating all things—all love, all beauty, all life-force. Subtly it captures, and delineates in music of weird loveliness, that tired, tortured terror of the world and its denizens that Mrs. Stone has come to feel, though eventually to embrace.

The Quintero direction never falters. The photography is in handsome, muted color, delicately appropriate to mood and setting, catching the myriad lovelinesses of the Roman environment and the juxtapositions of the characters with poetic aptness.

Vivien Leigh, right

Vivien Leigh and Jeremy Spenser (in mirror)

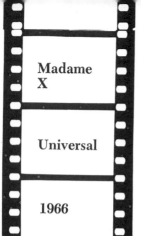

Madame X

Universal

1966

CREDITS: Directed by David Lowell Rich. Produced by Ross Hunter. Screenplay by Jean Holloway, based on a play by Alexandre Bisson. Color by Technicolor. Photographed by Russell Metty. Music by Frank Skinner. Art Direction by Alexander Golitzen and George Webb. Set Decorations by Howard Bristol. Assistant Director, Douglas Green. Gowns by Jean Louis.

OPENED at the Amsterdam and neighborhood theatres, New York, April 27, 1966. Running time: 100 minutes.

CAST: Lana Turner (Holly Parker); John Forsythe (Clay Anderson); Ricardo Montalban (Phil Benton); Burgess Meredith (Dan Sullivan); Constance Bennett (Estelle); Keir Dullea (Clay Jr.); Teddy Quinn (Clay Jr. as a boy); Virginia Grey (Mimsy); Carl Benton Reid (Judge); Warren Stevens (Michael Spalding); John Van Dreelen (Christian Torben); Frank Marth (Detective); Bryan Gross (Boy).

Lana Turner and John Forsythe

When Alexandre Bisson's play, *Madame X*, debuted back in 1909, it was considered pretty hot stuff. The lurid, melodramatic tale of a lady who lost husband, son and social position and descended "to the depths," as they used to say, murdered a blackmailer to save her husband and child from learning what she had become, then found herself defended in court by the son she had not seen since his early childhood, now a stalwart young defense attorney who labels the mysterious murderess "Madame X," was surefire entertainment for the time—and it proved mightily—and monotonously—durable through the years.

There were four Screen treatments: the Pauline Frederick silent version in 1920, quite creditable for its time, the 1929 Ruth Chatterton talkie, the 1937 Gladys George rendition—and nearly thirty years after that none other than Miss Lana Turner joined the "Madame X" parade. This 1966 streamlined model came courtesy of producer Ross Hunter (who was retreading oldies long before Peter Bogdanovich got the idea).

Jean Holloway turned out a passable screenplay, considering that she was working against hopeless odds, namely the basic material and premise, and director David Lowell Rich did the best he could with it. And Mr. Hunter provided lavish Technicolor, gorgeous gowns and jewels for Turner, plus production values done up to the nines.

The hyperexpensive, overproduced, overdressed, overblown enterprise debuted in New York's neighborhood theatres in April 1966, all 100 minutes of it —and to read the reviewers of the time, there were 100 minutes too many.

The critical roasting of 1966 seems justified enough when "Madame X the Fourth" is viewed today. What was wrong? Many things. The story is simply too hackneyed, forced and impossibly romantic for audiences of the past twenty-five years, let alone the last ten. Gladys George got away with it in 1937 because that year was still fairly hospitable to romantic items of this particular persuasion. Miss George was also a better actress than Miss Turner and gave the role a tough, brittle realism (alternating with womanly tenderness when required) that redeemed the mediocre screenplay. Miss Chatterton had the benefit of the talkie novelty and with her

John Forsythe, Lana Turner and Teddy Quinn

Keir Dullea and Lana Turner

stage-trained voice made the most of it, though the plot wobbled suspiciously even in 1929—which really dates it. As for Miss Frederick, the lady was right on top of it, for in 1920 such stories seemed novel, daring, even exciting. In modern parlance, *Madame X* in 1920, "got it all together."

But to return to Miss Turner and Mr. Hunter and *their* version.

There is no denying that Miss Turner's real-life experiences have eminently qualified her for lurid roles in which she fouls up with the men and makes a mess of motherhood. She has always been a distinctly limited actress, but when she is handed a part where she can inwardly push a button, so to speak, and relive experiences and feelings with which she has an intimate real-life acquaintance, she can be surprisingly effective. She even copped an Oscar nomination for *Peyton Place* (1957) and since her character on-screen in that corresponded to much she had gone through over the years, she was per-

Virginia Grey, Ricardo Montalban, Constance Bennett, Lana Turner and John Forsythe

Lana Turner and Burgess Meredith, right

fectly dandy. Again in *Madame X*, she manages to wander through the mink and diamonds and sugary plot unrealities of the earlier sections with her mind obviously elsewhere, then surprises the viewer with a realistic, deeply felt courtroom scene. Her shock when she discovers that Keir Dullea is actually her now-grown son bravely defending her against a murder charge, was put across powerfully. And she expressed, in her tired eyes and forlorn bearing, all the world-sickness of a beaten, bewildered woman. As they say in Hollywood, "If Turner can *identify* with what she's playing, the current goes

on." In *Madame X* the current is on, but not often enough.

There is also a brittle, unbelievable performance by Constance Bennett, then sixty (she died before the film's release) as a witchy mother-in-law who seizes on Miss Turner's indiscretion with a man she accidentally killed, to maneuver her permanent severance from her husband, State Department biggie John Forsythe (in a wooden performance) who has political ambitions. In return for getting her out of a possible manslaughter rap, Bennett forces Turner to change her identity completely, disappear to

Europe—in short, get lost for keeps. Her death by "drowning" is duly reported in the papers and her husband thinks her dead.

After this a lost, miserable Turner has a thing with a concert pianist whose proposal she rejects for fear of bigamy. Then it's down-down-down, drugs, drinking, promiscuity, the whole bit. Black-mailer Burgess Meredith tries to put on the screws, and Turner kills him for his pains. Then it's on to the time-hallowed courtroom scene and her young defense lawyer, Keir Dullea, who manages to project considerable appeal into his unlikely role. Added unlikelihoods were perpetrated with an aged Bennett and graying Forsythe at the back of the courtroom watching the proceedings.

But during the trial Turner has the current on, in spades, and when her tired heart gives out she plays with young Dullea (who never learns she is his mother) a death scene in which (one suspects) Miss Turner put more than a little of her own real-life heartache, *Weltschmerz* and emotional turmoil.

A romantic film? For the past fifty or sixty years *Madame X* has been considered just that. Certainly it is romantic in its wishful thinking, in its juggling of dramatic situations to induce tears, vicarious purgations, meretricious sentiment and other varieties of audience response. And in a few scenes of the 1966 incarnation, Miss Turner does give the picture a strong claim to the adjective "romantic." As we noted in our *Stella Dallas* critique, mother-love has a built-in romantic component, and the glamorous unrealities of *Madame X* and Miss Turner's occasional realistic emoting (elements not as mutually contradictory as one might think) place it among the fifty "elect" of The Romantic Film.

Lana Turner and Teddy Quinn

Lana Turner and Burgess Meredith

The Loves of Isadora

Universal

1969

CREDITS: Directed by Karel Reisz. Produced by Robert and Raymond Hakim. Screenplay by Melvyn Bragg and Clive Exton. Based on the books *My Life* by Isadora Duncan and *Isadora Duncan: An Intimate Portrait* by Sewell Brooks. Screen adaptation by Melvyn Bragg. Additional Dialogue by Margaret Drabble. Photographed by Larry Pizer. Production designed by Jocelyn Herbert. Art Direction by Michael Seymour and Ralph Brinton. Original music by Maurice Jarre. Arrangements for classical music by Anthony Bowles. Edited by Tom Priestley. Sound by Ken Ritchie and Maurice Askew. Choreography by Litz Pisk. Titles by Barney Wan. Costumes by John Briggs and Jackie Breed. Makeup by Wally Schneiderman. Production Supervisor, Roy Parkinson.

OPENED at the Sutton and Orleans theatres, New York, April 27, 1969. Running time: 128 minutes. (Original running time: 177 minutes.)

CAST: Vanessa Redgrave (Isadora Duncan); James Fox (Gordon Craig); Jason Robards (Paris Singer); Ivan Tchenko (Sergei Essenin); John Fraser (Roger); Bessie Love (Mrs. Duncan); Cynthia Harris (Mary Desti); Libby Glenn (Elizabeth Duncan); Tony Vogel (Raymond Duncan); Wallas Eaton (Archer); John Quentin (Pim); Nicholas Pennel (Bedford); Ronnie Gilbert (Miss Chase); Christian Duvaleix (Armand); Margaret Courtenay (Raucous Woman); Arthur White (Hearty Husband); Iza Teller (Alicia); Vladimir Leskovar (Bugatti); John Warner (Mr. Sterling); Ina De La Haye (Russian Teacher); John Brandon (Gospel Billy); Lucinda Chambers (Deirdre); Simon Lutton Davies (Patrick); Alan Gifford (Tour Manager); and David Healy, Zuleika Robson, Noel Davies, Arnold Diamond, Anthony Gardner, Sally Travers, Mark Dignam, Robin Lloyd, Constantine Iranski, Lucy Saroyan, Jan Conrad, Hall Galilli, Roy Stephens, Cal McCord, Richard Marner, Stefan Gryss.

Jason Robards and Vanessa Redgrave

There has been much controversy over *The Loves of Isadora*, or *Isadora* as it was originally known. The original running time was 177 minutes, cut later to 128 minutes, and having seen (and a number of times) only the 128-minute version I cannot say what the original must have amounted to (nearly 50 minutes cut out of any picture, even a long one, is something to give any critic pause) but what I did see, I liked.

Isadora Duncan, the highly individualistic, romantically impressionistic dancer who lived, danced, worked, suffered, loved by her own code, may have irritated a lot of people along the way but it is safe to say she never bored anybody: temperamental bohemian, high priestess of modern dance, advocate of free love before such advocacies were fashionable —Isadora was quite something!

The film opens with the aging (forty-nine) Isadora dictating her memoirs to a companion and secretary in a small hotel on the French Riviera . . . as a girl in America she burns her parents' marriage certificate to show her disdain for convention, and announces that the Pursuit of Art and Beauty were her all-encompassing goals. She languishes in a music hall for a while but soon is on her way to England. Greek classicism is the style on which she models her free-form dance expression and apparel, and an arresting on-stage figure she makes. Soon she is internationally famous, not so much for her talent but for her individualism and flair.

In Berlin she meets her soulmate—for the time being—in Gordon Craig, the stage designer. They have a daughter, and ambitious plans for revolutionary staging that never come to much, after which it's Paris and the sewing-machine millionaire Paris Singer, who lavishes presents and money on her, as well as clothes and jewelry, the finest Paris—both Parises—can offer. At the great estate Singer buys her, Isadora opens what she calls a School for Life.

Simplicity, beauty, classical expressiveness are the key words. She has a son by Singer, becomes bored, has an affair with her pianist. Later her children are drowned when their car dives off a bridge into the Seine and this terrible scene, riveted forever in her memory, keeps recurring as a tragic-elegiac psychic *leitmotif* throughout the film.

By 1921 she is in Russia, on invitation, where

Vanessa Redgrave

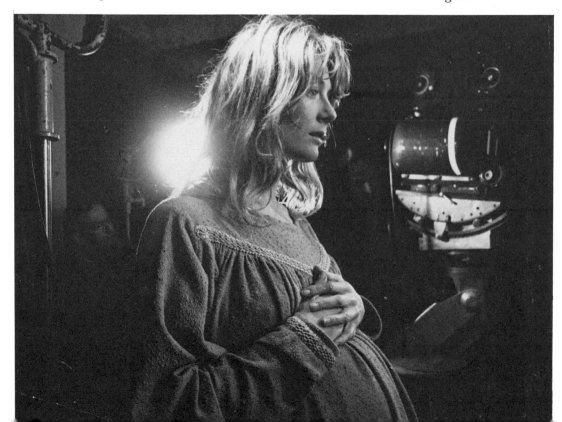

189

*Ivan Tchenko
and Vanessa Redgrave*

she is lionized by the Soviet peasants and soldiery who crowd around her while she dances in her inimitable style and chant, "I-sa-do-ra . . . Is–a–do–ra . . ." one of the picture's more arresting sequences. Next on the irrepressible, life-hungry Isadora's list of amours is Sergei Essenin, a young Russian poet who is as intense and passionate as she. They make a volatile pair, and she marries him so that he can obtain a visa to the United States. Here they plan a jamboree of expressionistic dance and Essenin-style poetics, but anti-Bolshevik sentiment in the United States, circa 1921, to say nothing of Essenin's boorish escapades, and capped by Isadora's breast-baring during a Slave Dance that is an excitement in its own right, send the two packing back to Europe.

Her marriage disintegrates, she wanders some more, sorrowing intermittently and obsessively over the two little lost ones of the Seine, then decides to sell what she has left to open a new school of dance in Paris. But in an attempt to reaffirm her love of life and excitement she goes to a cafe in Nice, there meets a young man who has taken her fancy for some time, and dances with him a wild, impassioned tango that brings onlookers to their feet in tribute to the old Isadora. But her scarf catches on the spoke of his wheel as they set off for a wild drive, and Isadora dies, her neck broken, in a freak accident.

Much of the film's entrancing luminescence is due to Vanessa Redgrave's interpretation: she is wondrous indeed, a woman of many sides and moods, her dances suggestive of the most uninhibited sex, exciting in their movements and imaginative turns. Watch her as she slithers and heels and dips, descends, ascends, her face transfixed with life-wonder,

love-hunger, sex-obsession. As Redgrave plays her, she runs like a sleek cat through life, wheeling and dealing, loving one man, manipulating another, chasing lost dreams and fostering short-lived causes; internationalist in scope, she cares not who is communist or democrat, monarchist or republican, poet or peasant, conservative or rogue—men are men—to be used as grist for her mill, be it physical, creative, or what-have-you.

The men she meets, romances, sometimes marries, and parts from in bewildering tandem are played by actors whose talents and suitability to their roles vary; James Fox is a mediocre Gordon Craig; Vanessa the Effervescent overwhelms him from the start, and Jason Robards, while sardonic and coolly subtle as Singer, seems a case of miscasting. Ivan Tchenko comes across best as the poet Essenin; he gives Miss Redgrave a real run for her money in the temperament-pyrotechnics department and the scenes in which he figures have a double liveliness as a result. John Fraser is patient and sustaining as the secretary and Vladimir Leskovar dances a tango opposite Redgrave that puts some real dynamics into the picture in the rousing sequence at the Nice night-spot just before her death.

Karel Reisz is a fine director for my money, though other critics don't seem to fancy him. He had a lot of territory to cover, and he guided the volcanic Vanessa and her stable of men, the frequent scenery shifts, the peregrinative excitements and variations of this on-the-go film in masterly style. The picture has élan, bite, excitement, great pictorial beauty, haunting music—and is in toto the quintessence of the romantic spirit gone absolutely and beautifully wild.

James Fox and Vanessa Redgrave

Teorema

Walter Reade-Continental

1969

CREDITS: Directed and Written by Pier Paolo Pasolini, based on his novel. An Aetos Film, Released in the United States by the Walter Reade Organization through Continental Distributing. Produced by Franco Rossellini and Manolo Bolognini. Photographed by Giuseppe Ruzzolini. Music composed by Ennio Morricone and conducted by Bruno Nicolai. Art Direction by Luciano Puccini. Edited by Nino Baragli. Costumes by Marcella De Marchis. Sound by Dario Fronzetti. Production Manager, Paolo Frasca. Assistant Director, Sergio Citti. Eastman Color, with U.S. Print by Movielab. English subtitles.

OPENED at the Coronet Theatre, New York, April 21, 1969. Running time: 93 minutes.

CAST: Terence Stamp (The Visitor); Silvana Mangano (The Wife); Massimo Girotti (The Husband); Anne Wiazemsky (The Daughter); Laura Betti (The Maid); Andres Jose Cruz (The Son); Ninetto Davoli (Angelino); and Alfonso Gatto, Carlo De Mejo, Adele Cambria, Soublette.

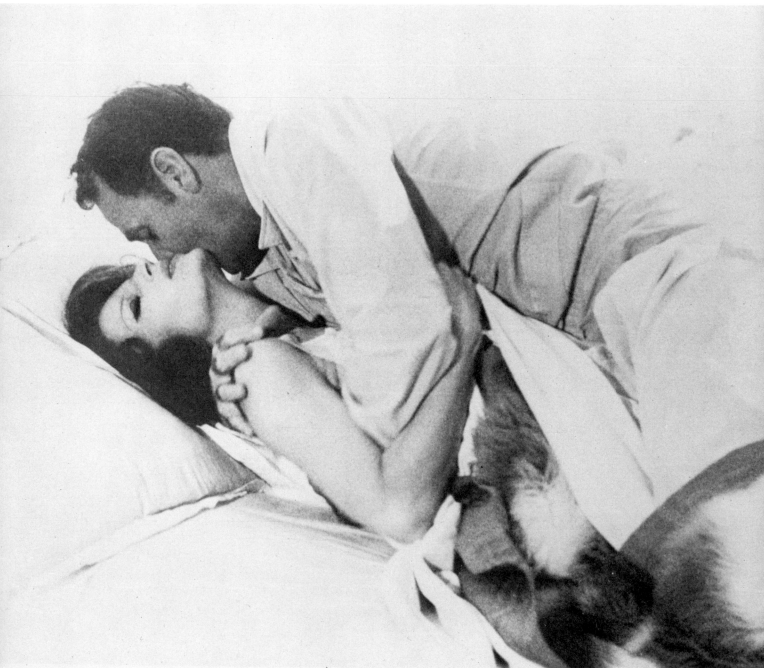

Silvana Mangano and Massimo Girotti

Terence Stamp

The director Pier Paolo Pasolini's distinctively mystic vision had one of its more exceptional workouts with *Teorema* (Theorem), the film he adapted from his novel. Pasolini and the Catholic Church had quite a run-in over this story, and he publicly mourned, "The old paternalistic spirit of the clerical Church, repressive and derogatory, is reborn after the brief parenthesis of Pope John." This after the Catholic Film Office had backtracked and withdrawn its award to the film.

And what was the film about? Well, it seems this very handsome and sexy young male creature appears out of nowhere in the household of a wealthy Milanese industrialist, and proceeds to soothe their sexual and emotional frustrations by making love to each and every one of them—the wife, who is so aroused by the experience that she is motivated to go out and pick up young men on the street, the husband, who ends up mooning over hustlers in railway stations and strips stark naked, winding up screaming his lungs out in what seems to be a desert environment, the son who once he has shared the Visitor's bed is inspired to go away and create abstract absurdist art on which he urinates to give it the final

Laura Betti

Laura Betti (top) levitating

Terence Stamp and Anne Wiazemsky

touch, the daughter, who is rendered catatonic by The Visitor's romantic ministrations and is carted off to an asylum in the deepest of trances.

And then there's the maid. Pasolini tells us that being of peasant stock, she is the only one in the household who understands the sacredness of this being who comes from another world, so she goes back to her village, levitates, works miracles and seems well on her way to beatification, if not canonization, by the picture's end.

The above, in a nutshell, is what *Teorema* is about, at least so far as plot goes.

It's obviously about much more: that the bourgeoisie have lost the sense of the sacred, being enmeshed in worldliness and unable to conceive and relate except sexually. That the Spirit of Truth, Beauty and Ultimate Spirituality which the handsome young man, well played by Terence (Billy Budd) Stamp, represents finds himself in an inhospitable, spiritually benighted world where only the elemental peasant understands the sacred and the betters of the universe can only ask, and whine, and plead, or rage, or go mad, or chase whatever sexual image turns them on.

194

Laura Betti

Like all artists, past and present, Pasolini has his own vision of the function of beautiful young men in the human esthetic scheme. They have appeared more often than not as Angels of Death—here Pasolini seems to be saying that this young man offers deepened insights, life-affirming principles, spiritually liberated and healthy insights, that those to whom he offers them are too much "with the world" to understand or appreciate.

The acting in *Teorema* is exceptionally fine. Silvana Mangano is tortured indeed as she seeks out young men in streets and alleys and makes love to them in their sordid little rooms and ditches situated beside churches. Redemption of a kind is forecast for her when she leaves her latest lover to go into a wayside chapel and stare at the sanctuary. She stares —and stares—and we can only hope she gets the results that, at long last, she seems to be seeking in the right quarters.

Massimo Girotti as the husband who repairs naked to the desert, Anne Wiazemsky as the nice girl gone catatonic, and Andres Jose Cruz as the urinating painter, are all true to their characters, and almost painfully sincere in their acting out of their assorted benightedments, or bedevilings, or possessions, or—you name it.

Teorema, for all its strangeness, at least offers a point—that mystic messages cannot get through if the self—and the soul—are depleted and desensitized by self-destructive adherences to the World, the Flesh and the Moneypot.

In this spirit, the film—and Pasolini—make their point.

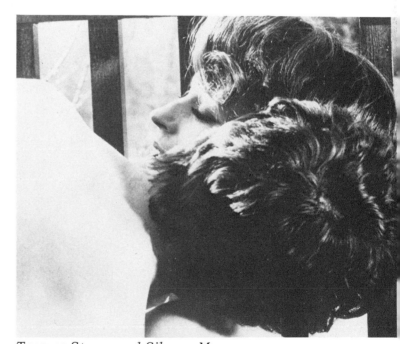

Terence Stamp and Silvana Mangano

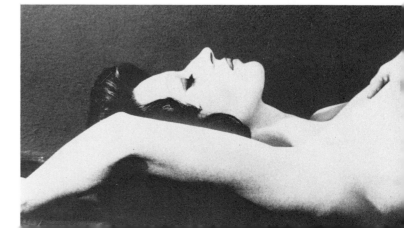

Silvana Mangano

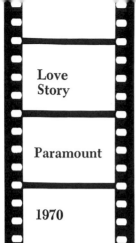

Love Story

Paramount

1970

CREDITS: Directed by Arthur Hiller. Written by Erich Segal. Photographed by Dick Krafina. Produced by Howard G. Minsky. Music by Francis Lai. Excerpts from Bach, Mozart, Handel.

OPENED at Loew's State and Tower East theatres, New York, December 17, 1970. Running time: 100 minutes.

CAST: Ali MacGraw (Jenny Cavilleri); Ryan O'Neal (Oliver Barrett 4th); Ray Milland (Oliver Barrett 3rd); Katherine Balfour (Mrs. Oliver Barrett 3rd); John Marley (Phil Cavilleri); Russell Nype (Dean Thompson); Sydney Walker (Dr. Shapley); Robert Modica (Dr. Addison).

Ryan O'Neal and Ali MacGraw

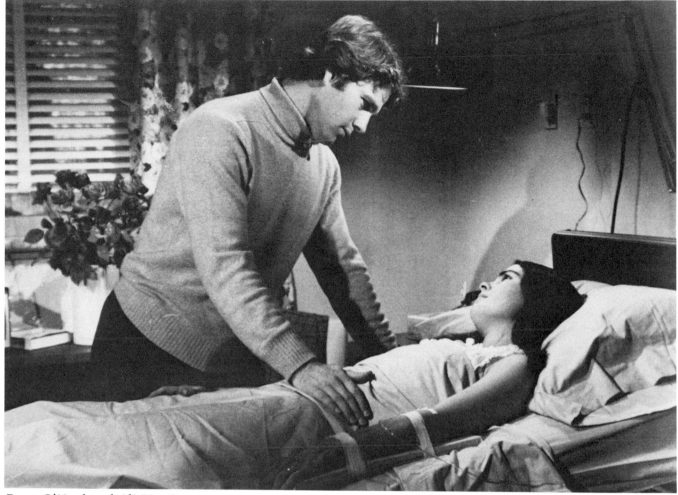

Ryan O'Neal and Ali MacGraw

"Love means never having to say you're sorry."

I have always felt that this inane and hollow assertion expresses much that is wrong with a picture that has as its chief claim to fame its heralding of the Romantic Return to a movie industry starved for it.

When Paramount producer Robert Evans was reproached by colleagues for taking a chance on it, on the grounds that "this isn't what today's market wants," he replied, "I'm not making films for today's market; I'm making films for tomorrow's market."

Tomorrow's, or yesterday's—where's the difference, you may wonder, but he assured that the film audience of the 1930s and 1940s who went to tender romantic fare were *not* accustomed to a rather masculine heroine who uttered four-letter words, as Ali MacGraw does in this, nor was stoical (or is it wooden?) Ryan O'Neal quite right as the sensitive aristocrat who goes to Harvard, falls in love with a poor Radcliffe girl (the daughter of an Italian baker from Cranston, Rhode Island, with the rather picturesque name of Jenny Cavilleri), romps with her in the stadium snow rather like Elvira Madigan, marries her, braves the disapproval of snobbish dad Oliver Barrett III, endures poverty with her, makes Law Review, moves to New York, goes into law practice—and then—presto chango scenario!—learns that his Jenny is dying of an incurable disease.

He then labors and lumbers and suffers with her through the final months, numbly obeys her final request—that he lie down on her hospital bed with her—tells her father the sad news—then goes out in the snow to meditate.

Now there's nothing wrong with the basic story —it happens all the time in real life—but the treatment is not the world's greatest, nor is Erich Segal

John Marley and Ryan O'Neal

197

Ali MacGraw and Ryan O'Neal

much of a writer. His dialogue is sparse, his humor banal, he lacks eloquence, passion, spirit.

Nor did audiences of the 1930s get their heroines served up as dry, sardonic, deprecating, and it comes as a shock, even in a 1970 movie, to hear a girl tell a fellow that the main reason she was attracted enough to date him was that "you have a good body"—whereupon O'Neal smiles a lynx smile that is too close to a leer to qualify for inclusion in a "romantic" film.

A good sample of Segal's writing would be the following:

"What can you say about a twenty-five-year-old girl who died? That she was beautiful. And brilliant. That she loved Mozart and Bach. And the Beatles. And me."

What does that say? Absolutely nothing.

A Casey Robinson of Warners' fame or a Donald Ogden Stewart of MGM renown would have had a lot more to say about the hero, the heroine, and all of *Love Story*, in fact. A romance that understates, that waxes laconic just when rhapsodies are called for, is suspect romance in my books, but *Love Story*

must be credited with triggering off a romantic revival that expressed itself within a year in far more lush and uninhibited fare (*The Music Lovers*) and far more depthful and mystic romanticism (*Death in Venice*), so it's an ill wind that blows nobody good.

Francis Lai, the musician who scored this film, works hard to inject the elegiac and the rhapsodic, and succeeds—indeed at times, Mr. Lai, with his love of Mozart, whom he imitates, and Bach, and other classicists, seems the one creative person connected with the film.

Mr. O'Neal, for all his boyish all-American smile, is still very much the one-dimensional Rodney Harrington of *Peyton Place*, and Miss MacGraw is too harsh, masculine, strident and cold a person to be discovered languishing in terminal illnesses.

Ray Milland is properly stuffy as Oliver III, and John Marley as the Italian father from Cranston is, not too surprisingly, the best in the picture. Possibly because he gives the impression that he believes it all, which is a triumph of his esthetic imagination over his acting experience and savvy.

Ryan O'Neal and Ali MacGraw

Ali MacGraw and Ryan O'Neal

The Music Lovers

United Artists

1971

CREDITS: Produced and directed by Ken Russell. A Russfilm Production. Executive Producer, Roy Baird. Screenplay by Melvyn Bragg. Based on the book, *Beloved Friend* by Catherine Drinker Bowen and Barbara Von Meck. Music conducted by Andre Previn. Played by the London Symphony Orchestra. Panavision. Color by Deluxe. Solo Piano, Raphael Orozco. "Porgi Amor" sung by April Cantelo. Photographed by Douglas Slocombe. Costumes by Shirley Russell. Production Manager, Neville G. Thompson. Choreography by Terry Gilbert. Art Direction by Michael Knight. Sets by Ian Whittaker. Edited by Michael Bradsell. Musical advisors: Michael Moores, Elizabeth Cardin.

OPENED at the Coronet Theatre, New York, January 24, 1971. Running time: 122 minutes.

CAST: Richard Chamberlain (Peter Ilyich Tchaikovsky); Glenda Jackson (Nina); Max Adrian (Rubenstein); Christopher Gable (Count Anton Chiluvsky); Kenneth Colley (Modeste); Izabella Telezynska (Madame Von Meck); Maureen Pryor (Nina's mother); Sabina Maydelle (Sasha); Andrew Faulds (Davidov); Bruce Robinson (Alexei); Dennis Myers (Vladimir); John Myers (Anatole); Joanne Brown (Olga); Alex Jowdoinov (Dimitri Shubelov); Clive Gazes (Doctor); Georgina Parkinson (Adelina); Alain Dubreuil (Prince in *Swan Lake*); Graham Armitage (Prince Balukin); Ernest Bole (Headwaiter); James Russell (Bolyek); Alexander Russell (Young Von Meck).

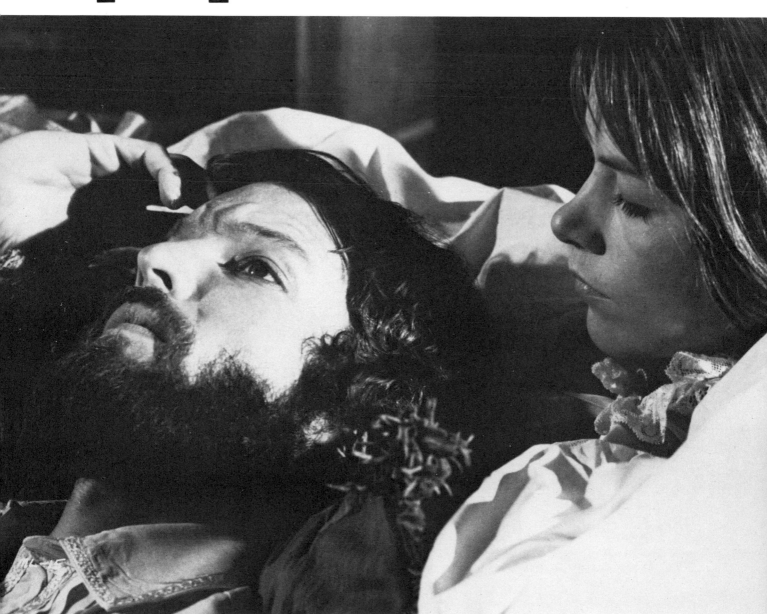

Richard Chamberlain and Glenda Jackson

Richard Chamberlain and Glenda Jackson

Ken Russell, whose art is as excitably romantic and unpredictably grotesque as the subjects he chooses to bring to the screen, is unquestionably a major talent. *The Music Lovers*, his individualistic, gorgeously sensual, hyper-cruel, racily uninhibited study of the life of the Russian composer Tchaikovsky, certainly raised a lot of dust, and got struck by a lot of lightning, all of it from reviewers who hated what they saw, called him disgusting, perverse, excessive. But not all critics were against him. Some pierced to the core of what this misunderstood genius was trying to do and say, and got the point—the point, at least in Russell's parlance, being that life is joyous, exciting, dark, radiant, electric—whatever the individual artist's mystique chooses to make it.

Let Russell speak for himself. About the time of *The Music Lovers'* release, he told an interviewer: "Of course (the picture) was excessive, crude, flamboyant; that was what fascinated me about the subject, the excessive romanticism . . . There seems to be a general distrust of freely expressed emotion these days—a feeling that there's a virtue in understatement. I don't believe that."

Glenda Jackson and Maureen Pryor

Understatement was certainly missing from *The Music Lovers,* nor would it have fit the subject or treatment. As everyone who cares about music—or enjoys prying into the lives of the famous of another day—knows by now, Tchaikovsky led such a grotesque life that it is difficult for any writer to exaggerate his peccadilloes, his lusts and hungers and sexual perversions. Many wonder how and when he ever got the time to compose the sublime music that has made him an immortal.

Richard Chamberlain plays Tchaikovsky. Christopher Gable plays his friend and lover, a rakish, dissolute young aristocrat. Then there is the Baroness Von Meck, played with restraint and melancholy dignity by Polish actress Izabella Telezynska, who becomes the composer's patroness on condition that they never meet. But there's no ban on correspondence, and the letters flood the post. The Technicolor is gorgeous, the production mounting sumptuous, the situations lurid and various, with Academy Award-winner Glenda Jackson on hand as the neurotic Nina, who marries a Tchaikovsky who represents a larger-than-life image to her (*he* marries *her* to escape the constant gossip about his homosexual amour with Gable). Obsessed with sex, mesmerized by his good looks and sensual body, Nina strips naked in their railroad compartment and writhes lustfully on the floor, sending the man of her choice up the wall. He continues to struggle with his homosexuality, runs wild with drink, sets himself up on an estate the Baroness provides, where he writes sublime music, presents it to her butler, then delights in secretly watching her open manuscripts that have flowers pressed in the pages (one of the few genuinely touching scenes in the film).

Meanwhile Miss Jackson's Nina has gone mad with the realization that Christopher Gable is a more attractive bed-partner to her man than she is. She turns prostitute, contracts syphilis, and ends up in an insane asylum where she writhes lasciviously on a grate while madmen grope from beneath—one of the film's more gamy scenes but in cinematic terms, fascinating. As for Chamberlain, he writes and writes, and writes, even after a bitchy Gable tells the baroness about his sexual predilections. She then deserts him and kills his subsidy. Not that he's really so badly off, you see, because things were getting pretty neurotic, what with her twin sons lifting him off beds (where the Baroness affects to lie chastely beside him without touching) and putting him out on the lawn to sleep in peace under a tree.

Then it's more music as before noted, and finally his recurring nightmare memory—of his cholera-stricken mother boiled in water—the standard cure of the day—catches up with him and in one final act of self-destructive irony he drinks water he knows is infected with cholera, gets the disease, and dies himself by the boiling-water treatment. You can make of that ending what you will.

A lot of talent went into this creative extravaganza, and that's the only term I can think of for it. Oddly enough, the so-called conservative Britishers loved it—it was running for months in London during the period I was there in 1971—but American reviewers were extremely crotchety, cranky and downright brutal about it, expressing their dislike in very strong terms.

What did I think of it? I loved it. I am not concerned with what was or was not telescoped, what year this or that occurred. I know enough about Peter Ilyich Tchaikovsky to note that the movie didn't exaggerate his life-style in its essentials.

Chamberlain, a really gifted actor, and Miss Jackson contributed wild, grotesque performances so luminous and volatile you can't take your eyes off them. Romance, yes—however excessive, however weird, Romance it certainly was.

Glenda Jackson and Richard Chamberlain

Christopher Gable and Richard Chamberlain

Death In Venice

Warner Bros.

1971

CREDITS: Produced and directed by Luchino Visconti for Alfa Cinematografica. An Italian-French Coproduction. Executive Producer, Mario Gallo. Associate Executive Producer, Robert Gordon Edwards. Screenplay by Luchino Visconti and Nicola Badalucco. Music by Gustav Mahler from his Third and Fifth symphonies, conducted by Franco Mannino. Based on the novel by Thomas Mann. Photographed by Pasquale De Santis. Art Direction by Ferdinando Scarfiotti. Edited by Ruggero Mastroianni. Sound by Vittorio Trentino and G. Muratori. Production Supervisor, E. Quarantotto. Production manager, Anna Davini. Costumes designed by Piero Tosi. Makeup by Mario De Silvio and Mauro Gavazzi. Miss Mangano's makeup by Goffredo Rocchetti. Miss Mangano's Hairdresser, M. T. Corridori. Hairdressers, Luciano Vito, G. DeGuilmi. Assistant Directors, Albino Cocco, Paolo Pietrangeli. Panavision. Technicolor.

OPENED at the Little Carnegie Theatre, New York, June 17, 1971. Running time: 130 minutes.

CAST: Dirk Bogarde (Aschenbach); Bjorn Andresen (Tadzio); Silvana Mangano (Tadzio's Mother); Mark Burns (Alfred); Romolo Valli (Hotel Manager); Marisa Berenson (Mrs. Aschenbach); Carol Andre (Esmerelda); Nora Ricci (The Governess); Leslie French (Travel Agent); Franco Fabrizi (Barber); Masha Predit (Singer); Sergio Garafanolo (Polish Youth); Luigi Battaglia (The Scapegrace); Ciro Cristofoletti (Hotel Clerk).

Marisa Berenson and Dirk Bogarde

Sergio Garafanolo and Bjorn Andresen

An unfairly maligned and misunderstood 1971 release, *Death in Venice,* like Brahms' "First Symphony" at its premiere, elicited a barrage of subjectively hysterical and blindly obtuse reactions from some American critics. The verdicts ranged from those which harped unduly on point-by-point comparisons with the Thomas Mann novella which is the source of Luchino Visconti's film to those which left the impression that the critic is so subjectively hypersensitive that he is afraid people will think he digs teen-age boys if he finds anything good in a film which deals, in poetic, metaphysical and *non*-sexual terms, with the obsessive love of a dying fifty-year-old composer for a singularly radiant and charismatic fifteen-year-old at a plush Lido resort in 1911.

I have always felt that this business of comparing book and film versions of a theme is overdone. The novel and the film are distinct and separate art forms. Why shouldn't what we see on the screen stand on its own? Mann is one kind of artist, Visconti another. Granted, then, the difference in the creative vision, just what does this film, *as a film,* reveal?

To begin with, Tadzio, the love-object of Aschenbach, could just as easily have been a girl as a boy; the homosexual implications are not really the main point. After all, women and girls have served to inspire artists in countless instances, and the delicacy, beauty and intrinsic truth of tales, poems, and paintings conceived by such inspirations are equally valid regardless of the specific sex of the inspirations.

In reading some off-base reviews of *Death in Venice,* I have been left with the feeling that some of these critics should be discussing their highly subjective impressions of this film with their analysts rather than with their reading public; this neurotic tendency to "witch-hunt" allegedly homosexual mystiques, be they real or imagined, indicates far more about the inner problems of the critic than it does about the film in question.

Other critics afflicted with private blind-spots have called *Death in Venice* boring, tedious, slow, devoid of action, pointless, without catharsis, etc.

Bjorn Andresen

All of which, I humbly suggest, indicates more about the shallowness and obtusity of the individual critic than about the intrinsic qualities of this superior film.

Indeed, after seeing *Death in Venice* twice in London (where the more sophisticated and discerning British critics accorded it rave reviews) and several more times in New York, I have come to feel that this picture offers to any perceptive analyst of human nature a peculiarly incisive "Rorschach test" of the individual viewing it. If he is shallow-minded, outer-directed, easily swayed by current cinematic fashions no matter how mindless and absurd; if he is easily beguiled by the cult of childish violence and nihilistic flounderings which pass for art in too many cinemas these days, he won't like *Death in Venice*. For this film is a deeply introspective masterpiece with subtleties that elude many

critics (and viewers) who have not cultivated self-awareness, do not know who or what they are or what life-principles they stand for—and hence, out of the baleful depths of their own vacuities, stand baffled, bored or irritated when confronted with the rare film that bids them *think*.

A true work of art elicits highly individual reactions. There is a beautiful, yet terrible, truth in *Death in Venice* that most people in our shallow, cacophonous American culture of the seventies are not conditioned to recognize, let alone face.

The youth Tadzio is many things: he is a symbol of truth, beauty and goodness, he is an esthetic image, he is the Angel of Death sent to guide this tortured, jaded, enervated, sickly, burnt-out, cruelly repressed fifty-year-old toward the ultimate consolations of Eternity. Gustav Mahler's haunting, evocative Adagietto from his "Fifth Symphony," repeated over and over throughout the film, along with selections from his "Third Symphony," are most apposite choices, for they are ravishingly mystical, deeply philosophical works. They help to illuminate the subtle points about age, sickness, death, eternity, the ultimate meaning of life, that Mann in his novella and Visconti in his film are making—Mann the austere *philosophe*, Visconti the lush romantic, aiming via different routes, for the same end result: illumination of truth and beauty.

Death in Venice takes its time. Its points are not made via hurried editing and pacing and flashy, pointless photographic techniques that stupidly deify (as so many foolish films do) style over content. In the first half it moves with a deliberately measured pace, and that is as it should be. Statements worth making need to be painstakingly established in proper settings and contexts, and moreover require sufficient time and a proliferation of subtle-ingredients-subtly-mixed, for ultimate impact.

Death in Venice is *not* a story about a pretty teen-ager and a dirty old man. It is superficial to carp

Silvana Mangano, Bjorn Andresen and Dirk Bogarde

Dirk Bogarde

about "nothing happening," "lack of confrontation," "absence of catharsis." For here we are faced with a complex and sophisticated *mood piece*, relentless in its pursuit of esthetic truth. The boy and the man never converse; why should they? Their unique communion is not based on the banalities of social intercourse, nor is it founded on coarse physicality. As the pitiful Aschenbach, tears in his eyes, sweat pouring from his brow, follows his young Beatific Vision through the plague-infested streets of Venice, while small fires rage and disinfectant is poured on the pavements, he mirrors the ultimate frustration of the artist, the tragic human truncations and shortcomings that hobble aspirations toward ultimate loveliness and mystical truth.

Some shots of Bjorn Andresen, the Tadzio of the film, could be extracted from the frame and hung on the walls of the Louvre or the Vatican in Rome. For this is not a pretty youngster who is supposed to represent an object of perverted lust; that was neither novelist Mann's nor director-screenwriter Visconti's intention. Rather, this is a symbol of a beauty allied to those which inspired Michelangelo's David and Da Vinci's Mona Lisa, and which moved Dante to seek ultimate esthetic catharsis in the distant figure of Beatrice.

Dirk Bogarde

Luchino Visconti instructs Dirk Bogarde during scene at Hotel des Bains on the Lido, Venice

Tadzio has been dispatched to Aschenbach by a kind of Overfate, to bring the dying man a capacity for fresh esthetic response that (as is stressed in the flashbacks) he has not been able to summon in his music, which his friend has castigated as "stillborn." The youth is, in effect, a double agent; he brings belated artistic insights to the stultified musician, and thus provides the ultimate justification for Aschenbach's existence. Tadzio then ushers Aschenbach into Eternity, for his time has come, his life arrived at full-circle. Down through the centuries, and in more than one art form, a handsome youth has symbolized the Angel of Death, or indeed Death itself. At the close of the film, as the dying Aschenbach yearns toward the mystical apparition, Tadzio, who walks into the ocean in dappled sunlight, the boy turns back toward him and raises his hand in the form of a circle, to symbolize that Aschenbach's departing spirit is to soar through that small circle into the all-embracing radiance of the sun.

Dick Bogarde, always an admirable performer, outdoes himself in this film; the part has met the man. Here is a singularly gifted actor at his finest hour, at the top of his form; indeed so convincing is he in the role that one gets the feeling that he believed in his character with a deeply felt intensity and identified with it thoroughly. The other performers are well cast, especially young Andresen as Tadzio and Silvana Mangano as his mother. The photography is exquisite and the editing shrewd.

Of all the films we saw that year, 1971, *Death in Venice* was the only one to strike authentic mystical chords. It was the one film that reaffirmed life by suggesting to us world-distracted souls that the best might yet be. A film that offers a sincere vision of the eternal, and suggests ultimacies of beauty and truth is to be cherished. In this respect, among the many ambitious films of 1971, *Death in Venice* stood alone.

Bjorn Andresen and Dirk Bogarde

Dirk Bogarde

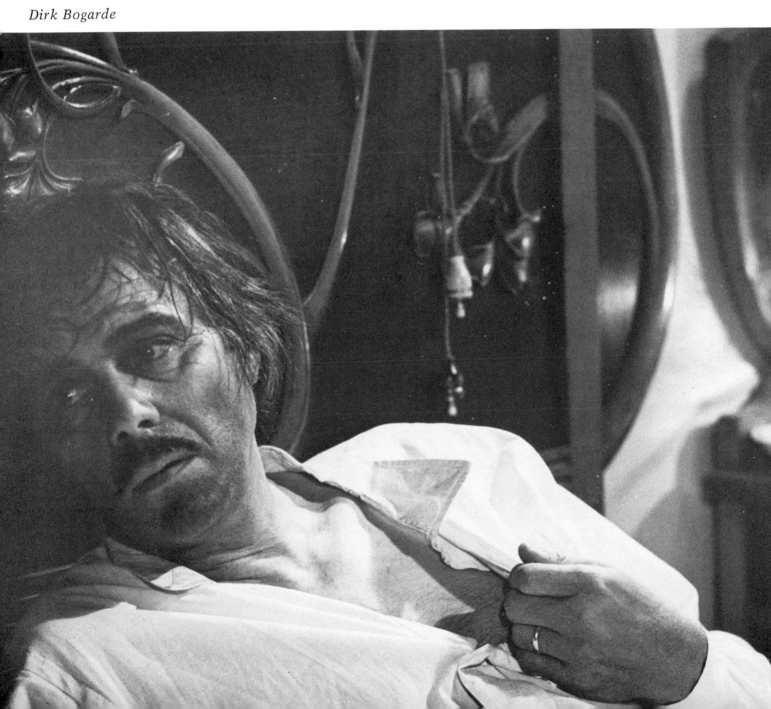

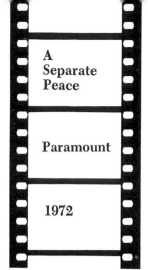

A
Separate
Peace

Paramount

1972

CREDITS: Directed by Larry Peerce. Produced by Robert Goldston and Otto Plaschkes. Screenplay by Fred Segal, based on the novel by John Knowles. Photographed by Frank Stanley. Art Direction by Charles Rosen. Music by Charles Fox. Edited by John C. Howard. Eastmancolor.

OPENNED at the Cinema II, New York, September 27, 1972. Running time: 104 minutes.

CAST: John Heyl (Finny); Parker Stevenson (Gene); Peter Brush (Leper); Victor Bevine (Brinker); Scott Bradbury (Chet); John E. A. Mackenzie (Bobby); Mark Trefethen (John); Frank Wilich Jr. (Quackenbush); William Roerick (Mr. Patchwithers); Elizabeth B. Brewster (Mrs. Patchwithers); Edward Echols (Mr. Ludbury).

John Heyl (center). Victor Bevine and Parker Stevenson (right)

Parker Stevenson and John Heyl

A Separate Peace, though far from the best film of 1972, was certainly one of the most puzzling and intriguing—and by allusion and implication, almost in spite of itself, one of the most romantic. We cannot agree with Rex Reed's gushy insistence that it is the best youth film ever made. I doubt that youths would understand it too well, though possibly they like its mirroring (even 1942-style mirroring) of youthful flounderings—but that doesn't make it a good "youth film."

No, there are deeper meanings to *A Separate Peace*, for it contains a secret—no, two secrets. Secret One: *What* motivated John Knowles to write a novel so passionately and deeply felt that it mesmerized millions of readers for years? Secret Two: *Why* did Gene knock his best pal and roommate Finny out of that tree? What was the real reason he did it, the real, deep-down, gut reason?

Now Knowles's novel, compared to director

Parker Stevenson and John Heyl

Parker Stevenson

Larry Peerce's and screenwriter Fred Segal's movie, is like a howling winter gale compared to a light spring breeze. Only Charles Fox's sensitive, apposite musical scoring reproduces the emotional atmosphere of the original. The filmmakers offer but a pale whisper of the author's bellowing intensity. The gay set, of course, has read all sorts of homosexual stuff into the close relationship between Gene and Finny, the most celebrated prep-school pals since David Copperfield and Steerforth, and granting that the gays often read their own wish-fulfillments into everything, they may in this instance be on target.

For even to an objective, dispassionate viewer

of the film, it is played like a love story, complete with Brahms-influenced mood music. And the novel itself reads like a passionate homosexual romance, though in actuality nothing overt occurs—but the language, the style, the intensity, implies much. Knowles was, after all, writing circa 1959, when, allowing for renegades of the era like Gore Vidal, subtlety was the watchword where this theme was concerned. But take passages like the one in which Gene, standing at his pal's burial, recalls it as his own funeral, and the famous and much-debated scene at eventide when blond-extrovert-pursuer Finny tells brunet-introvert-pursued Gene that in adolescence the one to be alone with on the beach at night is one's best pal, and Gene starts to reply in kind but, according to Knowles: "Something held me back. Perhaps I was stopped by that level of feeling, deeper than thought, which contains the truth." Followed by Gene's statement, later in the book, that "this must have been my purpose from the first, to become a part of Phineas." This certainly seems to indicate some homosexual attachment.

As for the tree incident, everything points to Gene's homosexual love-hate conflicts, which at sixteen frightened him, causing the fall of Finny at the hands of his best buddy—the fall of valor in the soul, as Charles Jackson would have had it. Gene was really the fallen one who sought to exorcise his pal's domination of his life and thoughts by symbolically emasculating and reducing him with a broken leg.

John Heyl and Parker Stevenson, amateurs with, however, confident and clear personality projection to their credit, offer the correct cinematic images of Finny and Gene respectively, and they are well supported by types who fit into Knowles' original dream-scheme. The character of Phineas (Finny) is perhaps the most panegyrically conceived and lovingly detailed of any by a novelist in this century—and it is significant that none of Knowles's subsequent novels approached his Finny portrait, which is what *A Separate Peace* essentially is.

No, Finny, luckily for his place in American literature, is drawn with deeply felt power and depth. Which disposes of *that* secret, both secrets in fact. But the movie version, compared with the novel, is sterile, self-conscious, choked up, frightened stiff of the truths staring it in the face, anxious to adhere to the straight, narrow and safe. But even a viewing of the teasingly timid movie would inspire any halfway bright person to want to reexamine the novel to resolve that persisting puzzlement—and then you realize that Mr. Knowles wrote a homosexual love story that puts Ryan O'Neal and Ali MacGraw and *their* love story in the shade. We are confronted, like it or lump it, with Finny, the All-American Loverboy whose strength is as the strength of ten because his heart is pure, in puppyishly innocent pursuit of Gene, who is not so pure, and who, despite his physical and emotional hungers, is a cautious, self-protective, independent-style weasel who turns on, and destroys, what he subconsciously loves but simultaneously regards as a threat to his wholeness and individuality.

And so Finny dies, by love released and Gene lives on, by love possessed, and makes that haunted, obsessed, heart-hungry, bedeviled return fifteen years later to the school to stare at the blackened hulk of tree that symbolized the Death of Love.

John Heyl, Victor Bevine and Parker Stevenson

Victor Bevine and Parker Stevenson

Parker Stevenson and John Heyl

Love and Pain

and the Whole Damn Thing

Columbia

1973

CREDITS: Produced and directed by Alan J. Pakula. Original story and screenplay by Alvin Sargent. Associate Producer, Thomas Pevsner. Art Direction by Enrique Alarcon. Edited by Russell Lloyd. Photographed by Geoffrey Unsworth, B.S.C. Production supervised by Roberto Roberts. Production Manager, Luis Hernanz. Assistant Director, Miguel Gil. Makeup by Mariano Garcia Rey. Hairdressing by Antonia Lopez Sanchez. Camera Operator, Peter MacDonald. Continuity by Angela Allen. Sound editing by Tom Simpson. Sound recording by Derek Ball and Nolan Roberts. Miss Smith's wardrobe designed by Germinal Rangel and made by Mitzou. Wardrobe Supervisor, Tony Pueo. Music composed and conducted by Michael Small.

OPENED at the Embassy 72nd Street and Columbia 1 Theatres, New York, April 19, 1973. Running time: 110 minutes.

CAST: Maggie Smith (Lila Fisher); Timothy Bottoms (Walter Elbertson); Don Jaime De Mora Y Aragon (The Duke); Emiliano Redondo (The Spanish Gentleman); Charles Baxter (Mr. Elbertson); Margaret Modlin (Mrs. Elbertson); May Heatherley (Melanie Elbertson); Lloyd Brimhall (Carl); Elmer Modlin (Dr. Edelheidt); Andres Monreal (Tourist Guide).

Maggie Smith and Timothy Bottoms

Timothy Bottoms and Maggie Smith

This is a pleasant, yet poignant, romance of a blighted, bumbling youth and an introverted, lonely older woman who meet while touring in Spain. It opened in New York in the spring of 1973 in quick playoff dates, and had *Love and Pain and The Whole Damn Thing* managed to survive in theatres long enough to attract the inevitable word-of-mouth that would have won a larger audience for its whimsical charm and moving love story, it might have become something of a cult phenomenon.

The distinguished English actress Maggie Smith, an Academy Award-winner for *The Prime of Miss Jean Brodie*, and young Timothy Bottoms, who at twenty-two is one of the more promising American talents, made an unusual but fetching romantic duo under the directorial aegis of Alan J. Pakula, who has brought out the best in his stars. Walter Elbertson, the character played by Bottoms, is a pathetic dropout, the cowed, apathetic son of a famous father, who sums up his background as: "I've been to a psychiatrist and I have asthma and my father won the Pulitzer Prize."

Lila Fisher (Miss Smith) is a reclusive, aging spinster, prim, fearful of losing her dignity, fearful of being hurt, fearful of exposure to feeling—in short fearful of life itself. Bottoms is clumsy and cloddish, and only half-alive due to a wounded self-image and the lack of understanding and love.

He abandons a bicycle tour and jumps on a bus. Maggie Smith is sitting next to him, and that is how they meet. She finds smudges from his chocolate bar on her dress; she gets locked in an outhouse, he goes to rescue her and they find themselves all wound up in flying toilet paper as they struggle back to the bus. When he does his laundry at a hotel, his shorts fly in her window and she primly relays them back via a movable clothesline. He flounders about listlessly and clumsily. She struggles with a strange lack of coordination which, it turns out, is a symptom of a terminal illness. Desperate and lonely, she bumbles with pills and wine and tries to kill herself; he rescues her and sits watchfully in her room all night.

After a night of wine and flamenco dancing in a

Maggie Smith and Timothy Bottoms

Timothy Bottoms and Maggie Smith

Spanish cafe, he makes a coltish pass, which she rebuffs. When, in despair at his own gauchery he rams his fist through her wall from his neighboring room, she tends his hand and again they try making love. She wrestles with her loneliness and despair—and so does he with his—and finally through a process of poignant trial and error, they wind up in each other's arms, and everything for once goes right, tenderness and meaning come into their world, and two blighted lives are transformed.

They travel on through Spain, through wondrous countryside, in a little car and trailer, and gradually he matures into a confident and purposeful young man, loved and loving. She glows with a new-found beauty and womanliness. And then he learns that she will die. She leaves him, he goes back to America, the blight once more apparent in his features and manner. But Love will not be denied, and he seeks her out for a return to Spain and a peasant wedding. They have decided that a short period of happiness is better than no happiness at all.

That is the basic plot of a film that originally bore the tenderly sardonic title *The Widower*. It was photographed in 1971, but not released for nearly two years. It is a picture filled with beautiful Spanish atmosphere, and the music by Michael Small is gentle, allusive, wistful, perfectly blended with a film which combines riotous humor with a haunting sadness.

Love and Pain was filmed in the Verona Studios in Madrid, and on such locations as Manzanares El Real, Colmenar de Oreja, El Escorial, the Royal Armory in Madrid and the castle of El Quexical near El Escorial.

Some talented actors supported the stars. Don Jaime de Mora y Aragon, a real-life Spanish aristocrat, plays a duke who rescues Miss Smith when she falls down a hill and later tries to make love to her. Whereupon she flees back to Bottoms, who has developed a bad case of jealousy. Emiliano Redondo plays a fey Spaniard who tries to woo Miss Smith with birdcalls. Charles Baxter is properly obtuse and self-involved as Bottoms's father and Lloyd Brimhall as the bicycle-tour leader registers convincing astonishment when he finds later in the picture that his client Bottoms under the influence of true love has blossomed from bumbling bleakness into self-confident warmth.

The injection of "the Ali MacGraws"—meaning the terminal illness of the heroine, as in *Love Story*, into a love story that didn't need it at all, occasioned some criticism when the film was released, with the writer castigated for not leaving well enough alone. Certainly it is a charming love story, one that courses along poignantly and merrily on its own terms, marred only by extraneous minor elements such as the duke's attempted seduction. As a study of two people who overcome heartbreaking flaws of outlook, character, personality, and age difference, to communicate finally and completely, the film is enormously winning, with a low-keyed tenderness

Timothy Bottoms and Maggie Smith

Timothy Bottoms and Maggie Smith

all its own. Geoffrey Unsworth's photography catches the many sides of that enchanted land, Spain, and some shots of Miss Smith and Bottoms by fountains and lakes achieve a rhapsodic intensity thanks to Unsworth's creative compositions.

Miss Smith offers a complex, many-sided and deeply moving delineation of a dying middle-aged woman who finds love almost too late. And Bottoms, of *Johnny Got His Gun* and *The Last Picture Show* fame, reveals himself as one of the more sensitively gifted young screen actors, embroidering his equally complex role with detailed expressions, mannerisms and nuances that establish him as a serious artist in the making.

Love and Pain and the Whole Damn Thing is an authentically romantic film, an interesting harbinger for the future of the genre, its sadness leavened by humor, its sentiment colored by unexpected vivacities. Despite plotting flaws and superfluous elements, it was one of the more worthy offerings of 1973.

Maggie Smith and Timothy Bottoms

Timothy Bottoms; Spanish dancer with Maggie Smith

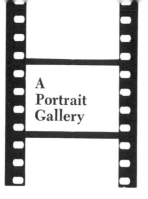

A
Portrait
Gallery

Vanessa Redgrave

Jane Wyman

Lana Turner